FRANCE

TIME-LIFE BOOKS/AMSTERDAM

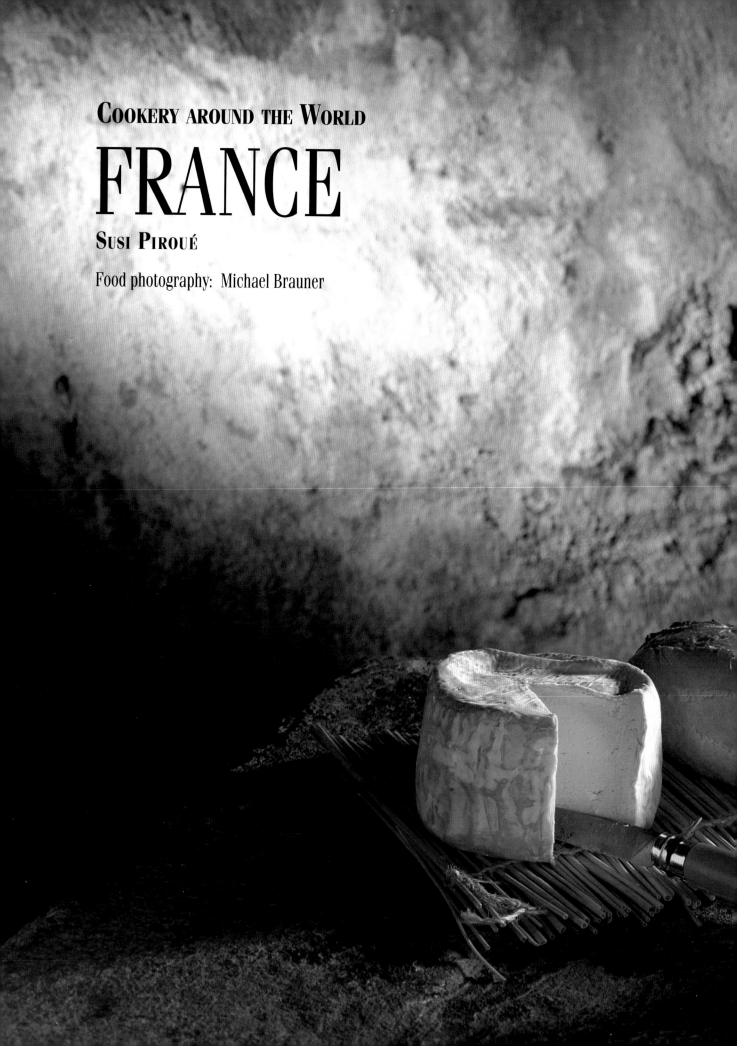

COOKERY AROUND THE WORLD
FRANCE

Susi Piroué

Food photography: Michael Brauner

Artois

Pica

Normany

Seine

Brittany

Anjou

Touraine

Loire

Vendée

Poitou

Berry

Aunis

Angou-
mois

Limousin

Saint-
onge

Bordelais

Dordogne

Périgord

Garonne

Gascony

Basque
country

Béarn

Roussillon

Spain

Par

Île-d
Fran

CONTENTS

FRANCE: HOME OF FINE CUISINE

French cookery is a byword for refined and sophisticated dishes, and for a rich variety of sauces. France gave the world *haute cuisine* and more recently, *nouvelle cuisine*; and it is the home of the very finest wines. Such is its influence that the very language of food is French: chef, restaurant, gourmet and cuisine itself.

But the grand tradition is only part of the story; there is an equally strong history of regional cuisine from the French provinces. Shaped by history and geography, this cookery is as varied as the landscapes of the country. And that is varied enough, including as it does sun-drenched Mediterranean shores; a cool, misty north; snow-covered mountains; and fertile plains.

Wherever you are, a saying goes, you can live like god in France, from storm-swept Brittany, savouring crêpes accompanied by cider, to sunny Provence, enjoying a bouillabaisse fragrant with herbs and washed down by red *vin ordinaire*. Each region has its own styles of cooking and its own specialities, which are sometimes distinguished from similar dishes elsewhere by the addition of just one local ingredient—a handful of shallots, say, in the Loire area. Everyday recipes have been handed down through families and improved from generation to generation.

What unites these different provincial styles, and classic *haute cuisine*, is a distinctive approach to cookery. The best, freshest ingredients available are prepared in ways as simple as they are refined. Seasonings are used to enhance rather than disguise the tastes of the basic ingredients. Above all, French cookery is characterized by the enthusiasm of the people themselves. The French are renowned as much for their savoir vivre as for their savoir faire—they have mastered the arts of enjoyment, first among which is the art of fine dining. An exuberant spirit as much as a talent for cookery has shaped their cuisine.

An abundance of good wine has also been important in the development of this cuisine, both as a drink and as a characteristic ingredient in sauces and stews. France is the heartland of wine. Its vineyards produce a remarkable variety of wines—the widest in the world. They are as diverse as the landscapes that create them, from the damp Atlantic coast to the baked Mediterranean hills and the cool foothills of the Alps. Their quality varies from ordinary *vin de table* to the great vintages of Bordeaux and Burgundy, or the finest champagne. They are among the glories of the French table.

This book aims to introduce you to French cuisine and the country and people that have created it. The first chapter takes us on a tour of the different regions of France, their landscapes and inhabitants, their festivals and local specialities. Then comes the recipe section, arranged in the traditional order in which dishes would be found on a menu. There are soups and starters, meat and fish dishes, and desserts, plus useful step pictures to illustrate some of the more complicated techniques. There are recommendations for wines to drink with particular dishes, and suggestions for varying recipes. An introduction to, and boxes within, each chapter provide details about typical regional produce and ingredients.

The quantities given in the recipes are not over generous, because a French meal usually consists of several courses. French meals are traditionally accompanied by crusty, fresh bread, though nowadays vegetable or potato dishes are often served with meat or fish, rather than as a starter or a separate course.

At the end of the book you will find some suggestions for typical menus, to enable you to treat yourself and your guests to authentic French meals at home. A glossary explains less familiar ingredients and some important French culinary expressions. *Bon appétit!*

A NATION OF GOURMETS

The French take food seriously. In 1671, France provided gastronomy with its first martyr when the *maître d'hôtel* at the Chateaux de Chantilly ran himself through with his sword because he had not been able to provide enough food for a banquet in honour of the king. More recently, in the mid-1960s, a Parisian chef shot himself when the *Guide Michelin* downgraded him from two stars to one, and then to none.

Fine food and drink have been important in French culture since at least the first century BC, when the Romans began to cultivate the region's vast natural resources—they planted the earliest vineyards in what was then Gaul—and their cookery began to influence the more basic native fare. When the barbarian invaders known as the Franks overran the country 600 years later, they inherited the opulent eating and drinking habits of imperial Rome.

A second wave of Italian influence came in 1533 when Catherine de Medici, daughter of the renowned Florentine family, arrived to marry Prince Henri of Valois, later Henri II. Catherine brought with her her own Italian cooks, and introduced new delicacies and refined table manners to the French court.

There began a new era in culinary art, and this *haute cuisine* continued to develop in the kitchens of the wealthy until the Revolution of 1789, when the fall of the aristocracy forced hundreds of private chefs out of work. Many opened their own restaurants—a recent phenomenon—which became the new centres of cookery. By the 19th century, French chefs had elevated cookery to an art and a science, appreciated by a nation of informed gourmets.

Alongside the restaurant tradition, the cookery of the provinces also flourished. French cuisine today reflects both traditions. Food and drink are regarded as yardsticks against which the quality of French life is measured, and that is why the entire nation devotes itself to the preparation and enjoyment of meals.

French cookery is best understood according to the traditions of its old provinces. Since the Revolution, France has been split into many *départements* within political regions, but the former provinces have continued to preserve their identities and heritage. In general, it is these older divisions that shape the country's linguistic, cultural and gastronomic structure.

With a few minor exceptions, this book defines culinary areas by these provinces, although in some cases they have been extended to include smaller neighbouring areas.

Sun gleams on the domes of the Basilica of the Sacré-Cœur. From its hillside in Montmartre, the church—completed only in 1919—is visible all over Paris.

A stylish entrance to the Paris underground is a lasting reminder of the Art Nouveau movement that flourished around the turn of the century, when the Metro was built.

Central and Eastern France

Paris and the Île de France

Paris is one of the world's gastronomic capitals. Few cities rival its reputation for elegance and style, and fewer still match the quality of its cuisine. Its renowned restaurants and bistros are among the highest expressions of the art of French cookery. These are not limited only to *haute cuisine,* though Paris is its home: the city also offers some of the finest regional cooking from the rest of France. The capital has long attracted people from the countryside, and their influence has shaped its cookery as much as that of the grand chefs.

For fresh ingredients, Paris traditionally relied on the Île de France, a fertile basin of forests, orchards, pastures and market gardens surrounding the city. Once the original kingdom of the Franks, from whom it took its name, the region was for centuries the capital's larder, linked by a network of roads and railways to the central market at Les Halles. Market gardens on the outskirts supplied Paris with some of France's finest fruit and vegetables—carrots from Crécy, asparagus from Argenteuil, peas from Clamart, strawberries from the Bièvres valley, mushrooms called *champignons de Paris* from caves along the Seine. Some still do, but many have been swallowed up by the expanding city.

From the Seine and Marne came freshwater fish, and the woodlands supported rich supplies of game—only 55 kilometres from Paris, wild boar still roam the Forest of Fontainebleau. It was to hunt game that the early French nobility settled here, building the chateaux in whose kitchens cooks began to develop classic French cuisine.

The Île de France is also the city's dairy: to the north, Chantilly produces cream, and to the east lies Brie, home of a famous French cheese. Made from unpasteurized milk in large, flat wheels, Brie has a slightly nutty aroma and should be soft but not runny. The region also produces the smaller Coulommiers and the cream cheeses Boursin and Fontainebleau.

The Île de France produces little wine, although Paris has its own not very distinguished vintage, made in small quantities from grapes cultivated in Montmartre, where an October festival celebrates the harvest. Outside the capital, a springtime strawberry festival takes place at Marcoussis-Bièvre, and the Versailles festival held in May and June is popular with visitors.

Champagne

About 150 kilometres northeast of Paris lie the drowsy vineyards of Champagne, home of the world's most famous sparkling wine, which was created here at the end of the 17th century. Dom Pérignon, a Benedictine monk, discovered how to capture the effervescence released as the local wine fermented by using strengthened bottles with corks tied down by string.

Champagne grapes flourish in the chalky soil of a small range of hills around the towns of Reims, Épernay and Chalons. After being pressed, fermented, blended and refermented, the wine is left to mature in cellars cut deep into the chalk for at least a year— three years for vintage champagne. The region also produces the non-sparkling Coteaux Champenois wines.

In contrast to the light wine, the cuisine is hearty and substantial, based on root vegetables, cabbages, potatoes and meat. To the north, rich stocks of game can be found in the rolling hills of the Ardennes, and hunting is popular. Pigs and cattle provide the meat for *boudin*, a black pudding; *andouillettes*, which are sausages made from pork chitterlings; and Ardennes ham. The many rivers are home to pike and trout.

Lorraine and Alsace

Long disputed by neighbouring Germany, these regions reflect German influence and periods of domination as much as they do mainstream French culture. The two countries also meet in the local cuisine.

Lorraine rises gently on the western side of the wooded Vosges mountains, which divide it from Alsace. It is a land of grain fields and fruit orchards, with rich deposits of coal and iron. The area specializes in egg dishes, including the well-known quiche, a savoury egg custard tart whose name comes from the German *Kuchen*, or cake.

Decked with flowers, a timbered, high-gabled winery in Mittelwihr typifies the Germanic character of the wine towns of Alsace. A sign-posted 150-kilometre "route des vins" threads its way through the vineyards.

Smiling with pride, an Alsatian landlord carves a ham that has been baked in a pastry shell. Charcuterie is a speciality of Alsace, where "Seigneur cochon", or the noble pig, has a place of honour.

A young man uses a time-honoured method to carry grapes from the vines. The September "vendange", or harvest, attracts young people from all over Europe.

Alsatian cooking has an even stronger German flavour. Sauerkraut is a local speciality, for example; there is even a society of master chefs of la Confrérie de la Choucroute. And there is *kugelhopf,* a yeast cake made in a fluted mould. Strasbourg, the main town, is famed for its sausages, ham and *pâté de foie gras,* which is made from the enlarged livers of force-fed geese. Cattle in the Vosges produce the milk for the strong-smelling Münster cheese.

Alsace and Lorraine are known for drink as much as for food. Alsace is a major beer producer, and fruits from both regions are used for distilled fruit brandies—called *eaux-de-vie*—and liqueurs, such as kirsch, from cherries; *quetsch,* from blue plums; and *framboise,* from raspberries.

Alsace is one of France's main wine areas, celebrated by annual fairs in the black-and-white timbered medieval wine towns south of Strasbourg. The white Riesling grapes that grow here produce strong, dry wine. The Gewürztraminer grape, an Alsatian speciality, produces an outstanding dessert wine when left to shrivel on the vine so that its sugar is concentrated.

Franche-Comté and the Alps

From the Jura mountains on the Swiss border, Franch-Comté runs down to Lake Geneva, where the Mont Blanc range of the Alps rises into Savoy and Dauphiné. Patchwork fields cover the foothills and the snowy peaks—major winter sports centres—fall steeply to clear streams and lakes. Like the character of the people, the cuisine has been shaped by this mountain environment: it is robust but subtle.

The mountains are a storehouse of natural treasures, from the trout and crayfish in the streams and lakes to the wild morel mushrooms that grow in the woods. Mountain herbs are used to flavour local omelettes: at Les Andrieux, an omelette festival each February welcomes the return of the sun, after 100 days behind the mountains. Hunters go in pursuit of plentiful wild game, including deer and boar, and pigs raised in remote villages are made into exquisite air-dried ham and sausages.

The foothills are dairy country, supporting cattle whose milk, cream, butter and cheese are important local ingredients. In the well-known *Gratin dauphinois,* for example, they give potatoes a creamy density. Cheeses include semi-hard *reblochon* from Savoy and hard Comté—similar to Swiss Gruyère—from Franche-Comté.

The Jura holds a special place in French cuisine, however, not because of its food, but as the birthplace of one of the most influential of all French gourmets, the 18th-century writer Brillat-Savarin. Among his observations on food and cookery, he coined the saying, "Tell me what you eat and I will tell you what you are."

Arbois, site of a wine fair each June, is the centre of the Jura's wine region. This is the home of *vin jaune*—yellow wine, which derives its colour from maturing in oak for over six years—that goes well with strong mountain cheese or game. The wines of Savoy include tangy, delicate whites, subtle rosés and light reds similar to Swiss wines. The western edge of the Dauphiné is part of the Côtes du Rhône: its Clairette de Die, thought to be the world's oldest sparkling wine, is said to date back to Roman times. The region's most famous drinks, however, are not wines at all, but mineral water from Evian and the herb liqueur Chartreuse, first blended by monks in a remote Dauphiné valley.

The Mediterranean Coast

Provence
Baked by the Mediterranean sun and swept by the dusty north wind called the mistral, Provence is one of France's most distinctive regions. Its eastern boundaries lie in the Maritime Alps on the Italian border; to the west it includes

The 12th-century abbey of Baumes-les-Messieurs nestles in the tranquil foothills of the Jura. Beneath the wooded slopes, the sheltered mountain valleys provide prime agricultural land.

Rows of lavender bring geometric order to the rocky hills of Provence. Grown mainly for the perfume industry, the fragrant plant also nourishes bees that produce exquisite honey.

The River Loue flows through Ornans in the Jura. Birthplace of the 19th-century realist painter Gustave Courbet, the town featured in many of his canvases.

the salt marshes of the Camargue at the mouth of the Rhone; between are the crowded beaches of the Côte d'Azur; and inland are bleak rocky hills and picturesque towns. Provence has attracted visitors for over 100 years with its warmth, its intense light and its subtropical vegetation, and its unique character is reflected in its cuisine.

Provençal cooking looks south towards the Mediterranean countries as much as north to the rest of France. Olive oil from the trees that flourish in the dry hills, for instance, is used in place of the butter of the north for cooking. Garlic and tomatoes—the characteristic ingredients of dishes *à la Provençal*—also grow well, as do the sweet-scented herbs that perfume the high, sheltered inland valleys: thyme, oregano, rosemary, fennel, wild lavender and mountain savoury.

Fish, usually from the Mediterranean but from rivers too, appears in classic regional soups and stews such as bouillabaisse from Marseille and *borride*. Sheep graze the inland hills, originally for wool but increasingly for

lamb, and sausages and hams are common. Other Provençal specialities include snails, truffles and quail. Sheltered from the mistral by hedges of cypress trees, early vegetables and fruit flourish on the plains around Avignon, and vegetables are widely used in first courses such as the renowned ratatouille of tomato, courgette and aubergine. Dishes such as *Salade niçoise* and ravioli show the influence of neighbouring Italy on the eastern area around Nice.

Few great wines are grown here— a typical vintage was once described as "tarpaulin edged with lace"—but the light reds, whites and rosés complement local dishes. The robust, deep red Châteauneuf-du-Pape from the southern Rhône valley goes well with game and strong cheeses.

Traditions and festivals reflect the vivacious Mediterranean spirit. There is, for example, a lemon festival at Menton in February and spring flower carnivals in Toulon and Hyères. In Grasse, roses are celebrated in spring and jasmine in summer; and throughout the region there are lavender festivals and markets. The gypsy pilgrimage to Saintes-Maries-de-la-Mer takes place in May, while at Fréjus bullfights are part of the August grape and wine celebrations. Along the coast, there are fishing festivals and Lent is celebrated with carnivals, particularly in Nice.

Languedoc and Roussillon
Arcing west along the coast from the mouth of the Rhone to the Spanish Pyrenees and rising inland to the wild gorges and mountains of the Massif Central, lie the sunbaked provinces of Languedoc and Roussillon, or the "red

land". Their cuisine is their own, but influences from the south and west are strong. As in Provence, for instance, the Mediterranean is a rich source of fish, which proliferate in the placid saltwater lagoons along the coast.

The characteristic dish of Languedoc, however, is cassoulet. Said to have Roman or Arab origins, this is a hearty stew of meat and white kidney beans, and authentic versions differ from town to town, some featuring goose, some lamb or pork. Roussillon, source of the early fruits and vegetables called *primeurs*, specializes in paella and omelettes filled with green peppers, tomatoes and ham, which, like the popularity of bullfighting, testify to the influence of Catalonia, over the Spanish border.

Inland, where Languedoc rises to the Massif Central, sheep graze on the aromatic scrub of the Cévennes hills and the grey limestone plateaus of the Causses. The only animals that adapt to this harsh landscape, they have been at the centre of mountain life for centuries. From sheep's milk comes Languedoc's most celebrated product, Roquefort cheese. This piquant blue cheese is made in the hill village of Roquefort, whose limestone caves harbour the unique bacteria that form the cheese's blue mould. Sheep's milk from all over France is sent to mature here; only cheese made in the caves may bear the name.

Languedoc-Roussillon is one of the world's largest wine regions, founded when the Roman occupiers of Gaul discovered that vines flourished in the stony hills where nothing else would. The department of Hérault alone produces more than a fifth of all French wine. From the area of the southern Côtes du Rhône comes the strong, dry Tavel, France's most famous rosé, while Roussillon produces the sweet

In his characteristic French beret, a man studies the local newspaper on the Côte d'Azur. Nice, the coast's major resort, was until 1860 part of the Italian kingdom of Sardinia.

A fisherman harvests oysters from beds at Bourcefranc-le-Chapus, on the Saintonge coast near the Île d'Oléron. Algae in the water give oysters from the area a greenish colour and an outstanding flavour.

fortified wines Rivesaltes and Banyuls.

The bounty of the vine and of the sea are celebrated in local festivals. Highlights include the October wine fair at Montpellier and the fishermen's festival in the commercial port of Sète, held during August.

The Atlantic Coast

Gascony and the Pyrenees

Where the Pyrenees run down to the Atlantic coast, the cuisine has been shaped by mountains and sea, and by the influence of the Basques, one of Europe's oldest peoples. In the forested mountains and isolated fishing ports, they have preserved an independent culture: the red, white and green Basque flag flies everywhere, and many of the men wear the beret, a national symbol.

Dishes from the Basque country are characterized by piquant sweet red peppers, called Espelette peppers after a local village. Each October the people festoon their houses with strings of peppers to dry in the sun. Other specialities include the mountain staples of hams and sausages from pigs that roam the wooded slopes: *tripotch*

is a black pudding; *loukinkas* are garlic sausages, and the town of Bayonne gives its name to a ham that is mildly smoked, salted and rubbed with pepper. The Basques are great fishermen, catching tuna, sardines and swordfish in the Bay of Biscay. *Ttoro*, a fish soup, is a favourite dish.

In the central Pyrenees lies Béarn, the mountainous birthplace of Henri of Navarre, who in 1589 became King Henri IV of France, founding the Bourbon line that lasted until the Revolution of 1789. Henri's rallying cry of "a chicken in every pot" gained him much support among the poor. An appropriate speciality of Béarn is *Poule au pot*, boiled, stuffed chicken with vegetables, which is eaten all over France.

Also popular is *confit*, a method of cooking salted pieces of goose, pork or duck in the animal's own fat and preserving them, sealed in by the fat, in large pots. Goose fat, rather than olive oil, is the frying medium for the region.

In the foothills to the north lies the more agricultural region of Gascony, known to millions of pilgrims because of Lourdes, whose waters are said to produce miraculous cures. Gascon cuisine—based on chickens, guinea fowl, black turkeys, geese and ducks bred in the woodlands, and vegetables from the Garonne valley in the north— was the subject in 1740 of France's first regional cookbook.

The scattered vineyards of the southwest date back to the Middle Ages. Among the wines of Béarn are the whites Pacherenc du Vic Bilh and Jurançon, but pride of place in the region goes to Armagnac from

Gascony. The world's oldest brandy, Armagnac is matured in oak casks for 10 or 12 years before bottling.

The Basques' distinctive festivals include Corpus Christi processions in spring and, in August, festivals of ancient Basque sports such as wood-chopping and stone-lifting.

Bordelais

In Bordelais cooking the influences of the Mediterranean south and the Atlantic north combine to create a highly varied cuisine. Southern olive oil and garlic, for example, are much used, balanced by more northern ingredients such as shallots.

Behind the beaches that stretch from the Basque country—called the *Côte d'Argent*, or "silver coast"—lies the

Landes, a flat, sandy plain covered by one of Europe's largest pine forests. To the north the rivers Garonne and Dordogne converge and empty into the sea in the Gironde estuary, where the port of Bordeaux nestles sheltered from the Atlantic. North and west of the city lie mild, well-drained river valleys ideal for growing the renowned Bordeaux wines.

Local dishes often include red or white wine sauces or marinades, but the grape is not the region's only natural treasure. From the forests of the Landes come succulent wild mushrooms called ceps, while the immense bay at Arcachon is home to the finest oysters in France.

Above all, the Bordelais means wine. The area is the world's greatest

The peaks of the western Pyrenees tower 3,000 metres in the Bigorre region of Gascony. A mild, wet climate makes the lower slopes ideal for grazing livestock.

Bright colours enliven the harbour of St.-Trojan-les-Bains, a resort on the Île d'Oléron. A popular holiday destination, the island is France's second-largest after Corsica.

producer of fine wines, and the name of Bordeaux is synonymous with a fruity, robust red wine produced in famous areas such as Médoc, St. Emilion, Pomerol and Graves. There are also white wines from Sauternes, Barsac, Entre-Deux-Mers and, again, Graves.

The Médoc is home to expensive wines—including Margaux, Rothschild and Latour—classified according to a system of five classes, or crus, established in 1855. From Sauternes comes Château d'Yquem, one of the most famous sweet white wines. And the dry white Entre-Deux-Mers, from the area of the same name, is an ideal accompaniment to fish and the renowned local oysters.

The festivals of the Bordelais, like its cuisine, celebrate the vine. There is a world wine trade fair in June, while in September, harvest celebrations take place throughout the entire region.

Aunis, Angoumois and Saintonge

North of the Gironde estuary, Aunis, Angoumois and Saintonge cover a fertile plain of cereal fields and dairy pastures. Inland from the old port of La Rochelle lies the Marais Poitevin, a marshy area cut by small canals where peasants transport everything—including their cows—on punts.

Cow's milk, cream and butter are the basis of a rich local cuisine. The Atlantic Ocean provides the ingredients for many local dishes such as *chaudrée*, a fish soup, and *mouclade*, a dish of mussels and cream. Snails, known as *cagouilles*, are a particular delicacy.

The most renowned product of the region's vineyards is cognac, one of the world's greatest brandies. This distilled wine is produced around the town of the same name, where the buildings used to be stained black by

the fumes of evaporating brandy. The special oak casks in which it matures give it its amber glow.

Brittany and the Vendée

Behind long beaches and a wooded coast, the Vendée is a thinly populated area of fruit orchards and dairy farming. To the north lies the rugged peninsula of Brittany, where church steeples and even hats have holes in them to act as vents against the constant wind. Hard lives, isolation and a Celtic heritage have shaped an independent people here who consider themselves Breton rather than French, and preserve their traditional customs, costumes and cookery.

The food is sustaining and simple, the result of a harsh climate and poor land, where even the sea's bounty—oysters, crabs, lobsters and prawns, and fish for *cotriade*, the Breton

version of bouillabaisse—is hard won on the wild coast. Lambs are grazed near the sea so that their meat acquires a salty taste, a delicacy called *pré-salé*. Meat, however, generally comes second to fish in quality and importance.

Inland, the poverty of the past is still reflected in the dominance of subsistence foods such as beans and buckwheat, which is used in local *crêpes*—thin pancakes with a variety of sweet and savoury fillings. Other delicacies include Breton butter and sturdy ground vegetables such as cauliflowers and artichokes, which grow in tiny fields protected by earth banks from the wind.

Although southern Brittany is home to the popular white wine muscadet, the typical drink—as in neighbouring Normandy—is cider, made from apples or pears (also called perry).

A young Breton woman wears the traditional costume of black dress and white "coiffe", an elaborate lace headdress. Once regular attire for Sundays and market days, such clothes are now kept mainly for special occasions.

A carving of a married couple adorns the medieval town of Vannes in Brittany.

Normandy cows graze on the rich pastures above the white cliffs near Yport. The so-called "alabaster coast", carved by the sea into coves and chalk stacks, stretches 140 kilometres along the English Channel.

The abbey of Mont-Saint-Michel perches 90 metres above the sea off Normandy. Founded in 708, the Gothic abbey is now among France's main tourist attractions.

The North Coast

Normandy

The landscape of Normandy, a prosperous and fertile region, recalls that of southern England. Behind the long Channel coast, small farms and timbered houses are scattered among apple orchards and dairy pastures enclosed by dense hedgerows.

Milk, butter and cream from the white-and-liver Normandy cattle form the basis of the local cuisine. The region produces a quarter of French beef and dairy products, including soft Camembert cheese. The sea also has an important role, providing Dover sole for *Sole à la normande*—poached in cream—and mussels. A popular Norman dessert is apple pie, made with fruit from the inland orchards.

Major apple products include cider—the most important drink, as Normandy produces no wine—and Calvados, an apple brandy, also used in many sweet and savoury regional recipes to give a subtle apple aroma. A unique local drink is the *digestif* Benedictine, created at the abbey of Fécamp from 27 herbs and spices.

Flanders, Artois and Picardy

The northeastern corner of France is a land of beer drinkers and farmers. On the low horizons of the flat Flanders plain, where the clay soil is heavily cultivated, tall, red-brick Flemish bell-towers testify to the influence of neighbouring Belgium. To the south, in the gentle hills of Picardy, large farms grow wheat, potato and sugar beet.

The cuisine is simple and rustic, based on local ingredients: fish from the sea, lamb from the coastal dunes, sugar beet for cakes and pastries. The Flemish influence is apparent in dishes characteristic of lowland areas—beef stewed in beer rather than wine, and *hochepot*, a heavy meat stew.

Inland France

Burgundy and Lyonnais

Good wine tends to encourage good cooking, and Burgundy and the Lyonnais share fine wines and a cuisine that enthusiasts claim rivals that of Paris. Lyon, they say, is the true gastronomic centre of France; one claimed, "Parisians taste everything without tasting anything; the Lyonnais eat."

History and geography have enabled this cuisine to flourish. When Burgundy was a prosperous independent duchy in the 14th and 15th centuries, cookery was among the arts encouraged by the court at Dijon. Since the 18th century, the traditional cuisine of Lyon has been in the hands of the "mères", women who have handed down recipes and cooking methods from generation to generation.

Set in the very heart of the country, where the northern plain breaks into hills, the landscape is largely gentle apart from the wild Morvan, a rocky massif with waterfalls and thick woods. The plain, dotted with forests, old towns and Renaissance châteaux, is prime agricultural land. France's finest poultry comes from Bresse and its finest beef from the white Charolais cattle of Burgundy. The provincial capital of Dijon is famed for aromatic mustard. Pigs from the Morvan produce air-dried ham, and pork is the most important meat: pork fat is used for cooking and the charcuterie of Lyon—such as *rosette de Lyon*, an air-dried sausage—is renowned throughout France. Ham is baked in white wine with parsley, or jellied in aspic to make *jambon persillé*. Fruit and vegetables

flourish in the mild Lyonnais climate.

Freshwater fish from the rivers Saône and Rhône are used in local dishes such as *pochouse*, a fish stew enriched with bacon and white wine. Local red wine, however, is more commonly used, and not only in dark stews such as *Boeuf bourguignon* and *Coq au vin*. There is a red wine sauce designed to accompany eggs, and even a red wine soup.

The very name Burgundy stands for velvety red wines. The best come from the Côte d'Or—the 48-kilometre "slope of gold" facing the river Saône which enjoys some of the best wine-growing conditions in all France. Young Beaujolais from Lyon flows in such quantities that the city has been said to stand on three rivers: Rhône, Saône and Beaujolais. The Côte d'Or also

Deceptively lazy, the river Lot flows under a 13th-century bridge at Espalion in the Aveyron. On its way west from the Massif Central, however, the river's force has carved a deep valley in the limestone plateaus of the Causses.

Périgord geese queue for feeding.

Sun gleams on the Renaissance château of Chambord on the Loire, once home to the kings of France. With 440 rooms, Chambord—begun in 1519—is the largest of the many Loire châteaux.

Slender chimneys mark the abbey kitchen at Fontevrault-l'Abbaye in the Loire Valley. Unusually, the 11th-century abbey housed both sexes.

produces fine white wine, as does Chablis. Kir, a blend of *crème de cassis* blackcurrant liqueur and white wine, is named after a popular mayor of Dijon.

Naturally, Burgundy's main festivals concern wine. Each January, a winegrowers' festival is held in a different village; Dijon has a wine festival in summer, while in November the new vintage is celebrated by three banquets called the Trois Glorieuses.

Auvergne, Limousin and Périgord
The Auvergne in the Massif Central and the uplands of Limousin are France's rocky heart, a bizarre landscape of ancient volcanoes, craters, precipitous gorges and twisting rivers. As in other mountainous areas, the cookery is substantial rather than subtle. The Auvergne is home to salted hams, dried sausages and cabbages. The stony uplands of Périgord in the southwest support scrubby oaks which foster the area's best-known delicacies—black truffles. Other specialities include foie gras and ceps, while everyday cookery uses cheese and potato dishes, bacon and sausages, walnuts and chestnuts.

Périgord is also famous for its geese and ducks, and goose fat or lard is used for cooking rather than butter.

Limousin and the Auvergne are cattle-breeding areas. As well as beef and veal, the cows provide milk for Cantal, a tangy hard cheese resembling Cheddar, which is acknowledged as France's oldest, having been produced for more than 2,000 years.

The Auvergne is home to more mineral waters than wines, and apple wine comes from Limousin. Périgord, however, has several characteristic wines, grown in the scattered vineyards of the southwest: golden Monbazillac, and light Bergerac from the boundary with the Bordeaux region. Fresh, fruity, red Pécharmant goes well with the local goose and pork specialities.

Anjou, Touraine, Berry and Poitou
The 1,000-kilometre Loire meanders through some of the most fertile land in Europe, passing vineyards, pastures and elegant chateaux. Towards the sea, the Anjou plains support grazing herds of Cholet cattle and fields of cereal crops; while to the south are grown a wide variety of vegetables and fruits, including the famous Poitou leeks and Charentais melons. Nearer Paris, the vast wheat fields of the Beauce, first cleared by monks building Chartres cathedral, are the granary of France.

But it is the central valley, especially the area around Tours—the Touraine—which is the jewel of the Loire. Lettuce and spinach grow between protective rows of poplars, and markets overflow with the benefits from the rich alluvial soil and mild climate: giant asparagus, succulent mushrooms, glossy tomatoes and juicy fruits. The Loire and its tributaries are full of fish and the forests are rich in game, though overshadowed by the former royal hunting grounds of Berry on the upper Loire. Quail, partridge, red deer, rabbit and hare take pride of place here.

The north bank of the central valley produces most of France's sparkling wines except champagne. Vouvray is a fine white, while Chinon and Bourgueil produce very palatable reds. The best-known product of the region is Rosé d'Anjou; from Berry comes the fine Sancerre, and each May there is a wine festival in the town of the same name.

Corsica

Corsica is French only in a political sense: its culture and cuisine are unique. From the hilly interior—covered by dense, aromatic scrub called *maquis*—come kid, snipe, honey, and pork from crossbred domestic pigs

and wild boar. The island's ubiquitous herbs are used for seasoning, and in brandies and liqueurs.

Corsican red wines are dark and potent, whites range from dry to sweet, and the rosés are fresh and fruity. Peaches, cherries and apricots make delicate, sweet fruit wines.

Cheeses mature in a Corsican cheese factory (above). Made by hand by traditional methods, the cheese comes from the milk of sheep and goats, animals that can survive on the impoverished limestone slopes of the island interior (below).

SOUPS

S oup has a traditional role in French cookery. In the farmhouse, it might be a meal in itself, consisting of a broth made of leftover meat, vegetables or fish poured over dry crusts of bread. Or it might be served as the first course of a meal, depending on the menu. Meals with only a few courses generally do not include soup. When they do, the soup is served either as the first course or after a cold hors-d'œuvre. Wherever it comes, it is essential that it should complement the meal to follow.

The French have two main words for soup: *soupe* and *potage*. Both have historical origins. *Soupe*—a liquid dish garnished with meat, fish or vegetables, and sometimes also enriched with bread, rice or pasta— originally referred to a slice of bread over which a stock or a bouillon was poured. *Potage*, on the other hand, denoted food "cooked in the pot". Today, there are a number of different types of *potage*: *potages clairs* are clear bouillons and consommés; *potages liés* are made with cream, butter or eggs; *potages purées* come from puréed vegetables; while in *potages tailles* the vegetables are cut into pieces. The rich, smooth soups made by puréeing shellfish are called *bisques*, and those we call cream soups are usually referred to as *les crèmes*.

Potage Parmentier
Cream of potato soup

Simple • Many regions

Serves 4

350 g floury potatoes
3 leeks
salt
freshly ground black pepper
1 bunch chives
10 cl cream (see Note)

Preparation time: 30 minutes

670 kJ/160 calories per portion

1 Peel the potatoes and cut them into small pieces. Trim the leeks, discarding the green parts. Thinly slice the white parts and wash thoroughly.

2 Place the potatoes and leeks in a heavy pan with 75 cl water, and season with salt and pepper. Bring to the boil, cover, and cook over medium heat for about 20 minutes. Meanwhile, wash, dry and finely chop the chives.

3 Purée the soup in a blender or rub through a sieve. Return to the pan and stir in the cream. Heat through, but do not allow to boil.

4 Transfer the soup to a tureen and sprinkle with the chives. Serve very hot.

Variation: Chicken stock can be used instead of water.

Note: Double cream will make the soup dense and rich. Single cream will make a thinner soup, also rich but less heavy.

Potatoes

Spanish conquistadors introduced the potato to Europe from its native South America around 1570. Despite its popularity in countries such as Britain, however, it did not find favour in France for many years. The French considered it too strange to eat, preferring bread as their staple food. Shortage of bread was one cause of the unrest that sparked the overthrow of Louis XVI in the Revolution of 1789.

Ironically, Louis had done much to popularize the potato. A pharmacist called Antoine August Parmentier, commemorated in the name of many potato dishes, recognized the tuber's value as a food and launched a campaign in 1772 to introduce it to

his countrymen. He persuaded Louis to serve potatoes at court and the queen, Marie Antoinette, wore potato flowers in her hair. Despite the couple's fate, the potato was established as the country's most popular vegetable, used in dishes ranging from simple boiled potatoes to the more elaborate *Gratin dauphinois (page 58)*.

There are two main types of potato. The waxy varieties are the most suitable for gratins, potato cakes and plain boiling, while floury potatoes should be used for soups, purées and for chips.

Whenever possible, buy potatoes loose and unwashed, rather than prepacked in plastic. Green patches on potatoes are poisonous and must be carefully removed.

Potage Crécy
Cream of carrot soup

Not difficult · Île de France

Serves 4 to 6

400 g young carrots
1 onion
45 g butter
1 litre chicken stock
2 tsp tomato purée
2 tbsp rice
4 tbsp cream (see Note, page 26)
salt
freshly ground white pepper

Preparation time: 1 hour

**600 kJ/160 calories per portion
(if serving 6)**

1 Trim and wash the carrots and dice them finely. Peel and chop the onion.

2 Melt 30 g of the butter in a heavy saucepan. Add the onion and sauté over medium heat, stirring frequently, until translucent. Do not allow it to brown. Add the diced carrot, chicken stock, tomato purée and rice, reduce the heat to low and simmer, uncovered, for about 20 minutes.

3 Rub the soup through a sieve or purée it in a blender. Return to the pan and stir in the cream. Season with salt and pepper. Reheat, but do not let it boil. Add the remaining butter, transfer to a serving bowl or tureen and serve. If you like, garnish with thin strips of carrot, parboiled until soft.

Variation: Use beef stock instead of chicken stock, or fry 50 g diced bacon with the onions.

Note: Young carrots, generally available in summer, are small and bright orange; the taste is sweet. If you use older, larger carrots, peel them and cut up only the outer, orange part, discarding the woody centres.

Soupe de courge
Marrow and leek soup

Simple · Provence

Serves 6

600 g marrow
500 g floury potatoes
3 leeks
2 medium-sized onions
4 tbsp oil
60 g butter
salt
freshly ground black pepper
grated nutmeg
croûtons (optional · see Note)

Preparation time: 1 hour

930 kJ/220 calories per portion

1 Peel the marrow and remove the seeds. Peel the potatoes. Dice both vegetables. Trim and wash the leeks, peel the onions and thinly slice both.

2 Heat the oil and butter in a large saucepan. Sauté the sliced leeks and onions until transparent, without allowing them to brown. Add the diced marrow and potato and heat through. Add 1.5 litres hot water to the pan, and season with salt, pepper and nutmeg. Cover, and simmer for 15 to 20 minutes.

3 Rub the soup through a sieve or purée in a blender. Serve very hot.

Variation:
Potage au potiron (Pumpkin soup) Peel 1 kg pumpkin and cut into pieces. Boil in a covered pan in 30 cl salted water for about 20 minutes. Strain off the water and rub the cooked pumpkin through a sieve. Bring 75 cl milk to the boil and add to the pumpkin. Stir in 15 g butter and 10 cl cream. Season with a little sugar, nutmeg, salt and pepper. If you like, sprinkle the soup with croûtons.

Note: To make croûtons for a soup garnish, cut slices from a stale or firm loaf of bread, and dice them. Fry them gently in butter over low heat, tossing frequently, until brown and crisp on all sides. Drain well.

Bisque d'écrevisses

Crayfish bisque

Time-consuming • Many regions

Serves 6

100 g rice
salt
freshly ground black pepper
2 young carrots
2 small onions
200 g butter
1 garlic clove
1 sprig thyme
1 bay leaf
about 15 g parsley
a few stalks chervil
18 live crayfish
1 to 2 tbsp brandy
45 cl dry white wine
cayenne pepper
10 cl cream (see Note, page 26)

Preparation time: 1½ hours

1,900 kJ/450 calories per portion

1 Bring 25 cl water to the boil in a saucepan. Add the rice, and season with salt and pepper. Cook for 15 to 20 minutes, until the rice is tender but still firm; drain and reserve.

2 Meanwhile, trim, wash and finely dice the carrots. Peel and finely chop the onions. Heat 60 g of the butter in a saucepan and briefly sauté the carrots and onions. Peel and crush the garlic and add to the pan together with the herbs. Cook for about 15 minutes, stirring frequently.

3 Wash the crayfish. In another pan, bring plenty of water to the boil. Plunge in the crayfish. Cover, and simmer over medium heat for 5 to 10 minutes, until the crayfish turn bright red.

4 Drain the crayfish, add to the vegetables and cook briefly, stirring continuously. Gently heat the brandy in a ladle, light it, then carefully pour over the crayfish and flame briefly. Add a generous 75 cl water and the wine,

extinguishing the flame. Season with salt, pepper and cayenne pepper and continue to cook over low heat for about 5 to 6 minutes.

5 Remove the crayfish from the stock and allow to cool enough to handle. Remove the tails, peel them and reserve the flesh. In a mortar or food processor grind about half the crayfish heads and shells. Add the rice and pass through a food mill or sieve to remove any coarse shell fragments, moistening with stock if necessary. Add the resulting pulp to the stock and vegetables and heat through, stirring, over medium heat. Rub through a sieve or purée in a blender. Finally, pass the mixture through a cloth or fine sieve.

6 Return the soup to the saucepan and bring to a simmer over medium heat, beating with a whisk. Cut the crayfish tails in half and add to the soup. Remove from the heat. Stir in the remaining butter and the cream, transfer to a serving bowl or tureen and serve immediately.

Le mourtaïrol

Saffron soup

Serves 4

500 g mixed chicken offcuts (necks, wing tips, feet, etc.)
2 or 3 veal bones, or 1 calf's foot
soup vegetables—for example, 1 to 2 onions, 2 carrots, 2 leeks and 1 stick celery
1 bouquet garni
1 garlic head
200 mg powdered saffron
salt
4 thick slices crusty white or wholemeal bread

Preparation time: 2¼ hours

2,400 kJ/570 calories per portion

1 Thoroughly rinse the chicken offcuts and veal bones or calf's foot. Trim or peel and wash the vegetables.

2 In a large saucepan place the chicken offcuts, veal bones or calf's foot, vegetables, the bouquet garni and the garlic, together with 2 litres cold water. Partly cover, bring slowly to the boil and cook over medium heat for 1½ hours without stirring. From time to time skim any scum from the surface.

3 Strain the cooked broth through a sieve or colander lined with muslin. Allow to cool slightly and skim any fat from the surface, or blot it up with kitchen paper folded into layers.

4 Preheat the oven to 200°C (400°F or Mark 6). Dissolve the saffron in a small bowl with a few spoonfuls of the warm broth. Add to the rest of the broth and salt to taste. Arrange the bread slices in the bottom of an ovenproof casserole. Slowly pour over about half the broth, until the bread can absorb no more fluid, and place in the centre of the oven. Keep the remaining broth hot over low heat.

5 Bake the soup for about 30 minutes, adding a little more stock to the bread from time to time. Then remove the casserole from the oven, add any remaining stock and serve very hot.

Note: The broth—which can also be made using half a boiling fowl instead of the chicken offcuts and veal bones—can be prepared up to three days in advance and refrigerated until needed. This will also make it easier to remove the fat, which will solidify on the top.

Consommé aux profiteroles

Beef consommé with cheese puffs

More complex • Many regions

Serves 8

For the consommé:
1 leek • 1 large carrot
2 to 3 stalks chervil
250 g minced beef
2 egg whites
2.5 litres home-made beef stock
salt

For the choux dough:
30 g butter
salt • 60 g flour
20 g grated Gruyère cheese
1 egg

Preparation time: 1½ hours

800 kJ/190 calories per portion

1 Trim the leek and peel the carrot. Wash them and slice very thinly. Wash the chervil, pat dry and chop finely. Place the vegetables in a heavy saucepan, add the mince and the egg whites, and mix thoroughly.

2 Add the stock to the pan and bring to the boil, stirring constantly. Reduce the heat to low, cover the pan and simmer for about 45 minutes. The egg will rise to the surface, while the stock remains clear. Strain the consommé through muslin and salt it to taste.

3 Meanwhile, prepare the choux dough. Preheat the oven to 170°C (325°F or Mark 3). Melt the butter in a saucepan, add 12.5 cl water and a little salt, and cook over medium heat until the mixture foams. Remove from the heat and stir in the flour, cheese and egg. Return to the heat, stirring the dough with a wooden spoon until it thickens and comes away from the sides of the pan. Remove from the heat.

4 Grease or butter a baking sheet. Using two teaspoons, shape the dough into small balls about the size of a hazel nut and arrange them on the baking sheet. Bake in the centre of the oven for about 10 minutes, until the dough has puffed and turned golden-brown.

5 Serve the consommé hot with the cheese puffs floating on top.

Soupe à l'oignon

Onion soup

Simple • Paris

Serves 6

250 g mild onions
70 g butter
1 tbsp flour
salt
freshly ground black pepper
6 thin slices French baguette or crusty white bread
100 g grated Gruyère cheese

Preparation time: 1¼ hour

1,200 kJ/290 calories per portion

1 Peel the onions and chop very finely. In a heavy saucepan, preferably a copper one, heat 50 g of the butter and fry the onions very slowly until soft and golden-brown—about 30 minutes.

2 Sprinkle with the flour, and pour on 1.5 litres water. Stir, and season with salt and pepper. Cover the pan and simmer for a further 30 minutes.

3 Meanwhile, preheat the oven to its maximum temperature. Toast the bread gently in a dry frying pan or in the oven.

4 Pour the soup into individual ovenproof bowls. Place the bread slices on top and sprinkle with the cheese.

Top with flakes of the remaining butter and bake in the centre of the oven for about 7 minutes, until the cheese is brown and bubbling. Serve hot.

Variation: Just before serving, flavour each bowl of soup with 1 to 2 tbsp port or brandy. Instead of in the oven, the cheese can be browned under the grill.

Note: This renowned Parisian soup originated in the bars and brasseries of Les Halles, once the central market. It was a popular breakfast pick-me-up among early risers, while night-owls appreciated its reputation for dispelling the effects of alcohol: it is sometimes called drunkard's soup.

COLD
HORS-D'ŒUVRE

Even in the simplest of French homes, the hors-d'œuvre, which translated literally means "outside the work", is regarded as an indispensable prelude to the main business of the meal. Whether hot or cold, simple or elaborate, an hors-d'œuvre is designed to stimulate both the eye and the appetite, and to prepare the taste buds for the feast to follow. The variety of ingredients and dishes is infinite, their content dictated only by the season and by what is available in different regions.

In France, the main midday meal is usually preceded by a cold hors-d'œuvre. This may be a composed salad—green salads are served after the main course, to refresh the palate—a simple platter of cold meats, an array of vegetables dressed in vinaigrette or mayonnaise, or a sumptuous pâté. The components of such small dishes are always chosen with care: presentation is as important as texture and flavour.

Fresh, crusty bread and wine are the inevitable accompaniments to the hors-d'œuvre. Generally, a wine served with the first course should be lighter than that which follows with the main course; dry white wine, champagne, rosé or a light red are all suitable choices.

Crudités à l'anchoïade

Fairly easy • Provence

Raw vegetables with anchovy dressing

Serves 6

1 head celery
2 fennel bulbs
4 sweet peppers (2 red, 2 yellow)
2 heads chicory
2 lettuce hearts

For the dressing:
12 anchovy fillets canned in oil
4 to 6 garlic cloves, unpeeled
freshly ground black pepper
20 cl virgin olive oil

Preparation time: 1 hour

**1,700 kJ/400 calories per portion
(including dressing)**

1 For the dressing, drain the anchovy fillets and reserve the oil. Soak the fillets in water for about 30 minutes.

2 Rinse all the vegetables in cold water and drain. Trim the celery and cut into finger-length pieces. Trim the base of the fennel bulbs and remove any green stalks, leaving only the crisp white flesh. Cut this into thin slices. Halve the peppers lengthwise and remove the stalks, ribs and seeds. Cut into thin strips. Remove the outer leaves of the chicory and trim off the root end. Remove the hard core by inserting the point of a sharp knife about 3 cm into the base and cutting it out. Slice the chicory lengthwise into

strips. Pull apart the lettuce hearts and tear the leaves into bite-sized pieces. Arrange the prepared vegetables on 6 individual plates or all together on a large serving dish.

3 Boil the unpeeled garlic cloves in water for about 5 minutes. Slip off the skins then mash the flesh with a fork or crush with a pestle and mortar. Put the crushed garlic in a heatproof bowl in a *bain-marie (see Glossary)* or a double boiler. Add the anchovy fillets and cook for 20 minutes over very low heat. Season with pepper. Add the

reserved anchovy oil and the olive oil. Crush the anchovies with a fork and mix in thoroughly. Heat the dressing through and serve it warm with the raw vegetables.

Variations:
Carottes râpées

(Carrots with egg dressing)
Peel, wash and grate 250 g carrots. Separate the white and yolk of a hard-boiled egg. Mix the yolk with 1 tsp mustard, salt and pepper. Chop the white and stir into the mixture. Add 3 tbsp olive oil, then mix the dressing into the grated carrots.

Sauce rémoulade

(Herb Mayonnaise)
Place 3 egg yolks in a bowl. Season with salt and pepper and stir in 1 tsp wine vinegar or lemon juice and ½ tsp Dijon mustard. Whisking continuously, pour in ½ litre olive oil drop by drop until the mayonnaise thickens, then continue to pour in a slow, steady stream. Add 1 tbsp boiling water if the mixture is too thick. To flavour, chop 2 tbsp capers, 2 or 3 small gherkins and a bunch of fresh, mixed herbs (parsley, chives, tarragon, chervil), and stir in.

Remember to use only very fresh eggs from a source you trust for this sauce—uncooked eggs may carry the salmonella bacteria that causes food poisoning.

Terrine de poisson

Fish terrine

Serves 8

For the mousse:
500 g skinned fillets of fish (for example, half cod and half redfish, or a mixture of sole, whiting and hake)
2 to 3 egg whites
25 cl double cream
salt
freshly ground white pepper

For the terrine:
15 g butter
10 3mm-thick slices fresh salmon (about 400 g)
salt
freshly ground white pepper

For the vinaigrette:
2 eggs
1 tsp Dijon mustard
salt
freshly ground white pepper
3 tbsp mild white wine vinegar
10 tbsp olive oil
100 g fresh herbs (chervil, chives, parsley and tarragon)
2 tsp capers

Preparation time: 1½ hours (plus 2 to 3 hours chilling time)

1,800 kJ/430 calories per portion

1 Using a pestle and mortar or a food processor, crush the fish fillets to a thick paste. Add the egg whites and bind the mixture into a smooth purée.

2 Transfer the purée to a glass or metal bowl. Cover the bowl and stand it in a larger container filled with ice cubes or crushed ice. Leave in the refrigerator for 1 to 2 hours, until the purée is well chilled.

3 Remove from the refrigerator. If necessary, top up with more ice. Using a wooden spoon, stir the double cream into the purée a little at a time. Season with salt and pepper, and return to the refrigerator.

4 Preheat the oven to 180°C (350°F or Mark 4). Grease the inside of a 35 cm ovenproof terrine with half the butter.

Season the salmon with salt and pepper. Line the dish with the slices of salmon, arranging them so that they overlap one another and the ends hang over the edge (*above*).

5 Pour the chilled fish purée into the terrine and smooth down the top. Carefully fold the overlapping ends of the salmon fillets over the top. Spread the remaining butter on a sheet of greaseproof paper and cover the fish.

6 Stand the terrine in a roasting pan filled with 3 cm hot water. Cook in the centre of the oven for 35 to 40 minutes. Meanwhile, hard boil the eggs, plunge them in cold water to cool and shell.

7 Take the terrine dish out of the roasting pan and leave it to stand for about 10 minutes.

8 Discard the whites and mash the hard-boiled yolks with a fork. Season with salt and pepper and stir in the mustard, vinegar and oil. Wash, shake dry and finely chop the herbs and stir into the dressing with the capers.

9 Discard the greaseproof paper, place a plate or serving dish on top of the terrine (*above*), hold firmly in place and flip terrine and dish over together. Ease the mould gently off the terrine. Serve accompanied by the vinaigrette.

Wine: A light, dry white wine such as a Sancerre, Entre-Deux-Mers or Graves goes well with this terrine.

Note: To cool completely, refrigerate for about 30 minutes before serving. This terrine is also delicious served as a hot starter.

Asperges à la vinaigrette
Asparagus with oil and vinegar dressing

Not difficult • Lyonnais

Serves 4

1 kg green, or white, asparagus
1 tbsp lemon juice
sugar
salt

For the dressing:
4 whole eggs plus 2 egg yolks
(see Note)
20 cl virgin olive oil
10 cl good wine vinegar
1½ tsp Dijon mustard
2 tsp capers
4 tbsp red wine
salt
freshly ground black pepper
30 g parsley
few stalks chervil (optional)

Preparation time: 45 minutes

*2,900 kJ/690 calories per portion
(including dressing)*

1 Cut off the woody base of the green asparagus spears and peel the lower ends, or, if using white asparagus, peel the whole spears. Gently bind the spears together in small bundles with kitchen twine. Hard boil the whole eggs.

2 In a large, deep pot, bring plenty of water to the boil. Add the lemon juice, a little sugar and salt. Place the asparagus bundles in the pot, cover and cook over medium heat—about 8 to 10 minutes for green asparagus, or about 20 minutes for white—until tender. Gently remove and untie the asparagus, and lay the spears on kitchen paper to cool.

3 Separate the hard-boiled eggs. Finely chop the whites and set aside. In a bowl, mash the yolks with a fork and mix with the raw yolks. Stir in the oil,

vinegar, mustard, capers and red wine. Season with salt and pepper.

4 Wash and dry the parsley and, if using, the stalks of chervil. Chop finely and stir into the dressing, together with the chopped egg whites. Arrange the asparagus on a serving dish, pour over the dressing and serve.

Wine: Choose a fruity, strong white wine, such as an Alsace Riesling, to accompany this dish.

Variation: Asparagus is delicious served with just a simple dressing of oil, vinegar, salt and pepper.

Note: Use only very fresh eggs from a source you trust for this recipe— uncooked eggs may carry the salmonella bacteria that causes food poisoning.

Champignons à la moutarde
Mushrooms in a mustard dressing

Quick and easy • Loire Valley

Serves 4

500 g mushrooms
6 tbsp virgin olive oil
2 tsp Dijon mustard
salt
freshly ground black pepper

Preparation time: 25 minutes

650 kJ/150 calories per portion

1 Wipe the mushrooms clean with kitchen paper; if necessary, peel the caps. Trim the tips of the stalks.

2 Rinse the mushrooms briefly under cold running water, taking care not to let them absorb too much moisture. If you prefer, do not wash them at all.

3 Cut the mushrooms into fairly thick slices and place them in a bowl.

4 Whisk together the oil and mustard, and season with salt and pepper.

5 Pour the mustard dressing over the mushrooms and stir in carefully. Transfer to a serving dish.

Note: Use only crisp, fresh and preferably young—or button— mushrooms: the very white ones are particularly good raw. In France, these mushrooms, known as *champignons de Paris*, were cultivated commercially in limestone caves beside the Seine as early as the 17th century. Today they are extensively grown in the region of the Loire Valley.

Artichauts à la ciboulette

Not difficult • Brittany

Artichokes with chive dressing

Serves 4

4 artichokes
juice of 1 lemon
salt
2 eggs
1 large bunch chives
1 tsp Dijon mustard
6 tbsp virgin olive oil
1 tbsp wine vinegar
freshly ground black pepper

Preparation time: 50 minutes

1,500 kJ/360 calories per portion

1 Cut or snap off the stems of each artichoke and discard the tough outer leaves. Cut off the top quarter and any remaining hard tips. Wash under running water, separating the leaves slightly to remove any grit, then drop into acidulated water (*see Note*).

2 Bring plenty of water to the boil with the lemon juice and some salt in a large, non-reactive pan. Place the artichokes stem downwards in the water and boil, uncovered, over medium heat for about 40 minutes, or until tender. The artichokes are done if a leaf comes out easily when pulled.

3 Meanwhile, hard boil the eggs, plunge them into cold water to cool, then shell and finely chop. Finely chop the chives. Mix the mustard, oil and vinegar. Add the egg and chives and season with salt and pepper.

4 Remove the artichokes from the water, turn them upside down and drain thoroughly. Serve warm accompanied by the chive dressing.

Note: Artichokes react chemically with some metals and cut edges discolour when in contact with air; use stainless-steel knives, rub their cut edges with lemon juice or leave them in acidulated water, and cook in a non-reactive pan.

Artichokes

This distinctive vegetable, with its bunch of densely packed, olive-green "leaves" and delicate, nutlike taste is the unopened flower head of a perennial thistlelike plant. A native of North Africa, it was introduced to France from Italy during the 16th century by Catherine de Medici, who was so enamoured of the exotic delicacy that she claimed it would be the death of her. Today, artichokes are cultivated throughout France, Belgium and areas of the Mediterranean.

There are many different types of artichoke, varying in diameter from 5 to 13 cm, and in colour from pale green through to violet. The large, green Breton artichoke is a particularly popular variety.

Although immature heads can be tender enough to eat raw—sprinkled with salt or tossed in a salad—artichokes are generally eaten cooked. The edible parts are the heart and the base, arguably the choicest, and the fleshy inner base of the leaves, which are pulled off one by one and dipped in a sauce—such as a vinaigrette, hollandaise or mayonnaise.

Artichokes are available all year round and should be eaten as fresh as possible. Always choose the healthiest-looking specimens, with tightly packed leaves; open, spreading leaves indicate toughness. In spring, the leaves should be bright green—any discoloration is a sign of damage. Between November and March the leaves may be slightly bronzed due to frosting, but the flavour will nonetheless be good.

Salade niçoise

Nice-style salad

Serves 4

1 lettuce
3 spring onions
4 canned artichoke hearts
500 g fresh ripe tomatoes
50 g tuna canned in oil
24 black olives
3 tbsp virgin olive oil
1 tbsp good wine vinegar
salt
freshly ground black pepper
mixed fresh herbs (or 1 tsp dried herbs)

Preparation time: 20 minutes

810 kJ/190 calories per portion

1 Separate the lettuce into individual leaves, wash, and dry in a salad spinner. Trim, wash and slice the spring onions. Drain the artichoke hearts and cut them into quarters. Wash the tomatoes and cut them horizontally into thin slices.

2 Divide the lettuce leaves between four plates. Arrange the tomato, spring onion and artichoke quarters on top. Drain the tuna, reserving the oil, and break it up into flakes. Arrange the flakes on top of the tomatoes. Top with the olives.

3 Mix the oil from the tuna with the olive oil and vinegar. Season with salt and pepper and pour over the salad. Finely chop the mixed herbs and sprinkle over the salad.

Variations: Ingredients for *Salade niçoise* vary depending on the season and on what is available. Try chicory or frisée instead of round lettuce, and replace half the tomatoes with 2 yellow peppers, 2 sticks celery, 1 chopped Spanish onion and 2 hard-boiled eggs. Soaked and drained anchovy fillets, sprinkled over the salad, can be substituted for the tuna.

Œufs durs farcis vert-pré

Green stuffed eggs

Serves 4

4 eggs
6 spinach leaves
30 g parsley
2 sprigs fresh tarragon
10 chives
2 tbsp mayonnaise
1 tsp medium-hot mustard
1 tsp wine vinegar
salt
freshly ground black pepper
4 small gherkins
lettuce leaves

Preparation time: 25 minutes

1,000 kJ/240 calories per portion

1 Hard boil the eggs, plunge them in cold water to cool, then peel them. Meanwhile, remove the stalks and ribs from the spinach leaves, wash and pat dry. Wash and dry the parsley, tarragon and chives. Finely chop the spinach and herbs to make about 3 tbsp.

2 Mix the mayonnaise with the mustard and vinegar. Season with salt and pepper.

3 Halve the eggs lengthwise. Remove the yolks, chop them and stir into the mayonnaise. Stir in the chopped spinach and herbs.

4 Fill each egg half with a spoonful of the mixture. Slice the gherkins very thinly and garnish the eggs.

5 Wash the lettuce leaves and thoroughly pat dry with kitchen paper. Divide them between four plates and arrange the stuffed eggs on the top.

Variation: For the stuffing, mix 1 tsp mustard, 1 tbsp wine vinegar, 2 tbsp olive oil and 1 tbsp small capers with the hard-boiled egg yolks. Season with salt and pepper.

Note: Stuffed eggs are a very popular starter, easy to prepare and with many possible variations. They are also cheap and make an ideal first course for everyday meals.

Salade de crosnes

Fairly easy • Île de France

Chinese artichoke salad

Serves 6

500 g small waxy potatoes
salt
500 g Chinese artichokes, or
scorzonera (black salsify)
coarse sea salt
1 tbsp flour
1.5 kg fresh mussels
10 cl dry white wine
1 head celery
few stalks fresh tarragon

For the dressing:
8 tbsp olive oil
salt
freshly ground black pepper
2 tbsp sherry vinegar

Preparation time: 1 hour

1,300 kJ/310 calories
per portion

1 Boil the potatoes in their skins in salted water for about 20 minutes, until tender.

2 Meanwhile, lay the Chinese artichokes on a tea towel and sprinkle them with a handful of sea salt. Fold the towel over and rub vigorously to remove the dry skins. Rinse, then boil in salted water together with the flour for about 20 minutes.

3 In cold water, scrape, wash and beard the mussels. Tap sharply any that are open, and discard those that don't close. Bring ¼ litre water to the boil in a pan, add the mussels, cover and cook over high heat until the shells open. Discard any that remain closed.

4 Peel and slice the potatoes. Place them in a bowl, pour over the white wine and leave to cool. Drain the Chinese artichokes through a sieve.

5 Remove the leaves and stringy outer stalks of the celery. Trim the stalks and cut the heart into thin slices. Wash the tarragon and pat dry. Tear off the leaves and cut into small pieces.

6 Put the potato slices and the other salad ingredients in a large shallow serving bowl. Make a dressing with the oil, salt, pepper and vinegar, and pour over the salad. Carefully mix everything together. Serve warm or cold.

Note: Scorzonera, or black salsify, has a delicate flavour similar to globe artichokes or asparagus. If using, scrape or peel the scorzonera, dropping each one into acidulated water because they discolour quickly. Cut into lengths and, in a non-reactive pan, cook in boiling water with 1 tbsp flour for about 20 minutes.

Chinese artichokes

These curiously shaped yet exquisitely flavoured tubers are the horizontal underground stems of *stachys siboldii*. Between 5 and 7 cm long and 1 to 2 cm thick, their shape has been likened to a twisted shell or a pasta spiral.

The plant is native to northern China and Japan and was first introduced to France in the mid-19th century, where it was subsequently developed and cultivated, and from where it spread to the Americas. The tubers are esteemed for their delicate flavour by the French, who know them as *crosnes*, pronounced "crone", after the town in the Île de France where they were first cultivated.

Classic recipes cooked *à la japonaise* usually call for the inclusion of Chinese artichokes, which can be grated raw in salads, stir-fried in vegetable dishes or served as an accompaniment to meat.

They are less easily obtainable here but can be grown from tubers, available from good seed merchants. When buying Chinese artichokes, in season from autumn until spring, make sure you choose plump, light-coloured ones. Try to use them as soon as possible, as they quickly lose their moisture.

47

Terrine de foies de volaille

More complex · Lorraine

Chicken or goose liver terrine

Serves 6 to 8

500 g goose or chicken livers
250 g veal escalope
250 g pork escalope
300 g soft lard
2 tsp freshly ground black pepper
2 level tsp salt
½ tsp ground cloves
½ tsp ground ginger
½ tsp freshly grated nutmeg
4 cl brandy or Armagnac
few slices streaky bacon for lining
the terrine
1 bay leaf
1 to 2 sprigs thyme

Preparation time: about 2 hours
(plus resting and chilling time)

2,700 kJ/640 per portion
(if serving 8)

1 The livers and meat should be well chilled to make processing easier. Rinse the livers under cold running water, pat dry and remove green stains and connective tissues. Refrigerate 3 or 4 livers. Mince the remainder, together with the veal and pork escalopes, in a mincer or food processor.

2 Knead the lard into the minced meat (*above*), and add all the spices and the brandy or Armagnac. Place the mixing bowl in a larger bowl filled with ice cubes or crushed ice, and stir for about 10 minutes, until smooth. Cover, and leave to rest in the refrigerator for about 10 hours.

3 Preheat the oven to 220°C (425°F or Mark 7). Line a terrine with the rashers of bacon. Spoon in half the liver and meat mixture, and press down firmly to eliminate any air pockets. Arrange the reserved whole livers on top. Add the other half of the mixture (*above*) and press it down firmly. Place

the bay leaf and thyme on top of the terrine and put on the lid.

4 Fill a roasting pan large enough for the terrine to stand in with boiling water to a depth of about 5 cm. Place the terrine in the pan and place the pan at the bottom of the oven.

5 Cook the terrine for about 50 minutes. Check the water level from time to time, and top up with more hot water if necessary.

6 Ten minutes before the end of the cooking time, remove the lid to allow the terrine to brown lightly on the top.

7 The terrine will cut better if it is weighted before it cools. Cover it with a sheet of greaseproof paper, place a

dish or plate that fits inside the terrine on the paper, and put a weight on top (*above*). Allow to cool (*see Note*).

Wine: A light red wine, such as a Côtes de Provence, goes well with this terrine.

Note: To allow the flavours to mature and to make the terrine firmer and easier to slice, it is best to chill it in the refrigerator for 2 to 3 days (but 24 hours will suffice) before serving.

HOT HORS-D'ŒUVRE

I n France, hot hors-d'œuvre traditionally act as introductions to larger meals, usually in the evening, when they either replace cold starters or soups, or are served in addition to them. Because they are intended to stimulate both the eye and the appetite, these dishes are usually small and subtle. Often they consist of modest portions of delicacies such as wild mushrooms, or of foods such as vineyard snails, whose subtle flavours might be overwhelmed in the middle of a meal.

But the range of hors-d'œuvre also includes such versatile dishes as hot pâtés and terrines, omelettes and *crêpes*, quiches and flans in light pastry cases, vegetables fried in batter and baked savoury puddings. As well as being served as first courses, or—in more formal menus—after the soup before the fish or meat course, these can be eaten as snacks or smaller meals at other times of the day.

Although by tradition the French did not serve side dishes with meat or fish courses, nowadays vegetables or potato dishes, such as *Gratin dauphinois* (*page 58*) or French fries, are often used as accompaniments.

The wine should not be heavy. Depending on the dish, and the food and wine to follow, the French accompany hot starters with a dry white or light red wine, a rosé, or a glass of champagne.

Quiche au saumon
Salmon quiche

For the pastry:
250 g flour
125 g butter
1 egg yolk
salt

For the filling:
4 eggs
2 egg yolks
25 cl crème fraîche
grated nutmeg
salt
freshly ground black pepper
150 g smoked salmon
50 g butter

Preparation time: 1 hour
(plus 2 hours chilling time)

2,100 kJ/500 calories per portion
(if serving 8)

1 Sift the flour into a heap on a flat work surface and make a well in the middle. Cut the butter into small pieces and place in the well with the egg yolk, a little salt and 6 tbsp water.

2 With your fingertips, mix the other ingredients into the flour (*above*), working swiftly and kneading as little as possible, to make a dough that is smooth but not soft. (You may find it easier at first to use a knife to cut the butter into the flour.) If the mixture is too dry, add a little more water. Shape the dough into a ball, wrap in plastic film or foil, and chill for about 2 hours.

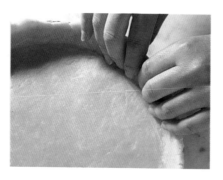

3 Preheat the oven to 200°C (400°F or Mark 6) and grease a 28 cm flan tin or springform tin with butter. Sprinkle the work surface with a little flour to prevent sticking. Roll out the dough to a thickness of about 4 mm, line the dish *(above)*, and blind bake the pastry (*see Glossary*) for about 10 minutes.

4 Meanwhile, to make the filling, beat the whole eggs and egg yolks with the crème fraîche. Season with nutmeg, salt and pepper. Beat once more, then pour into the pastry case. Increase the oven heat to 220°C (425°F or Mark 7).

5 Cut the salmon into thin strips and arrange on top of the egg mixture *(above)*. Dot with flakes of the butter.

6 Bake the quiche in the centre of the oven for about 25 minutes, or until the filling is golden-brown. After the first 10 minutes, cover the top with greaseproof paper to prevent the salmon from drying out. Allow to cool slightly. Serve warm.

Variation: Quiche Lorraine
Prepare the dough as in Steps 1 and 2 above. For the filling, finely dice 300 g smoked bacon and crush into it 2 to 3 garlic cloves. Beat 4 to 6 eggs in a bowl, add 200 g grated Emmenthal or Gruyère cheese, 20 cl cream, salt and pepper. Mix in the bacon and garlic.

Roll out the dough and line a greased 28 cm flan tin or springform tin. Blind bake (*see Glossary*) in a preheated oven at 200°C (400°F or Mark 6) for 10 minutes. Pour the filling into the pastry case and bake at about 220°C (425°F or Mark 7) for a further 30 minutes, or until golden-brown.

Soufflé au fromage

Cheese soufflé

Needs care • Franche-Comté

Serves 4

25 cl milk
50 g butter
50 g flour
grated nutmeg
salt
freshly ground black pepper
4 egg yolks
100 g grated Comté or Gruyère cheese
5 egg whites

Preparation time: 1¼ hours

1,500 kJ/360 calories per portion

1 Preheat the oven to 180°C (350°F or Mark 4). In a saucepan, gently heat the milk to a simmer.

2 Meanwhile, melt the butter in another saucepan and stir in the flour to make a roux. Remove from the heat and stir in the milk a little at a time. Season with nutmeg, salt and pepper, and cook over low heat for about 2 minutes, stirring constantly.

3 Remove from the heat, let the sauce cool for a moment, then briskly stir in the egg yolks and the cheese.

4 Beat the egg whites until very stiff, and fold into the warm cheese mixture.

5 Grease a 2 litre soufflé dish with butter and pour in the mixture.

6 Bake in the centre of the oven for about 45 minutes, until puffed and golden. Serve at once, or the soufflé will collapse.

Note: On no account open the oven door during the first 20 minutes of cooking. The soufflé is ready when its volume has about doubled.

Flan bourguignon

Leek flan

Not difficult • Burgundy

Serves about 6

For the pastry:
250 g flour
125 g butter
1 egg
salt

For the filling:
1 kg leeks
3 tbsp butter
1 tbsp flour
150 g cream
60 g grated Gruyère cheese

Preparation time: 1¼ hours (plus 2 hours chilling time)

2,300 kJ/550 calories per portion

1 Sift the flour into a heap on a board or worktop. Make a well in the middle and add the butter and egg with 2 tbsp water. Season with salt. With your fingertips, or a knife, mix the ingredients together, then knead gently into a dough, adding a little water if necessary. Roll into a ball, and chill for about 2 hours.

2 Preheat the oven to 200°C (400°F or Mark 6). On a floured surface, roll out the pastry to a thickness of about 4 mm. Butter a 28 cm flan tin or springform tin and line with the dough, pressing the raised edge to the rim. Blind-bake (*see Glossary*) in the centre of the oven for about 20 minutes.

3 Meanwhile, trim and wash the leeks. Discard the green parts and cut the white parts into small, very thin strips. Melt 2 tbsp of the butter in a heavy saucepan. Sauté the leeks in the butter until transparent, about 5 minutes. Sprinkle with the flour, stir briefly, then stir in the cream. Stir in 40 g of the cheese and remove from the heat.

4 Increase the oven temperature to 250°C (475°F or Mark 9).

5 Pour the filling into the pastry case. Sprinkle with the rest of the cheese and top with slivers of the remaining butter. Bake in the centre of the oven for about 15 minutes until puffed and golden-brown.

Wine: A fine, dry white Burgundy or rosé goes well with this dish.

Omelette aux tomates

Quick, but needs care • Périgord

Tomato omelette

Serves 4

4 very ripe tomatoes
1 onion
15 g parsley
2 tbsp oil
1 garlic clove
salt
freshly ground black pepper
6 fresh eggs
1 tbsp goose fat, or butter plus a few drops of oil

Preparation time: 25 minutes

1,400 kJ/330 calories per portion

1 Boil some water in a saucepan, plunge the tomatoes in briefly, drain, skin, deseed and cut into quarters. Peel and finely chop the onion. Wash the parsley, pat dry and chop finely.

2 Heat the oil in a saucepan. Add the tomatoes, onion and parsley. Peel the garlic clove, crush and add to the pan. Season with salt and pepper. Sauté over low heat for about 20 minutes, then remove from the heat.

3 Meanwhile, beat the eggs in a bowl. Add 1 tbsp cold water and season with

pepper. Continue beating until the mixture is evenly blended.

4 In a heavy frying pan, heat the fat or butter until it foams. Pour in the eggs and cook for about 30 seconds, until set on the edges. Then, with a spatula or fork, keep lifting the edges, tilting the pan to allow uncooked egg to run underneath. When the eggs are set but still very soft, pour on the tomatoes.

5 If you like, sprinkle with a little chopped parsley. Slide the omelette onto a warmed serving dish, folding it as you do so, and serve.

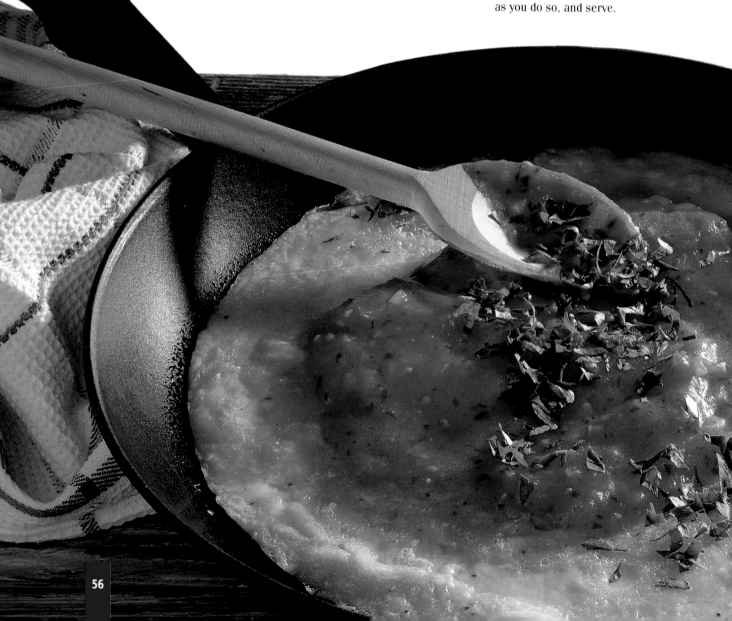

Omelettes

The omelette—a delicious dish of fried beaten eggs—is an ancient creation. Its name probably comes from the Latin *lamella*, meaning thin plate, and a Roman recipe exists from the first century AD. By 1400, French cooks were making omelettes similar to those we eat today.

The cooking technique lends itself to many variations—France is said to have more than 100 types. These range from rolled omelettes with savoury fillings to thicker cakes with vegetables stirred in; for a soufflé omelette, the whites are whisked separately, in others the eggs are enriched with cheese and cream.

For a classic rolled omelette, beaten eggs are fried in butter, oil or animal fat over high heat, and then may be folded over a savoury filling. The finished dish should be crisp on the outside and moist and light inside.

A few guidelines help ensure success. Use a heavy, flat-bottomed pan to ensure even cooking. Beat the eggs just before adding them to the pan. Make sure the fat is really hot before adding the eggs so that cooking is brisk and the eggs stay moist—a one-egg omelette should be set and ready to serve in less than a minute.

Gratin dauphinois

Not difficult • Dauphiné

Potato gratin

Serves 4

1 garlic clove
50 g butter
12 medium-sized waxy potatoes
salt
freshly ground black pepper
grated nutmeg
2 eggs
50 cl milk
2 tbsp double cream

Preparation time: 1 hour 20 minutes

1,800 kJ/430 calories per portion

1 Peel the garlic, cut in half crosswise and rub it round the inside of an ovenproof gratin dish. Then use a little of the butter to grease the dish.

2 Peel the potatoes, wash and dry them. Cut into very thin slices. Make a layer of potato in the bottom of the dish, overlapping the slices like tiles, and season with a little salt, pepper and nutmeg. Continue building up layers of potatoes, seasoning each layer.

3 Preheat the oven to 170°C (325°F or Mark 3).

4 Break the eggs into a bowl and stir in the milk and cream; whisk lightly with a fork. Pour the mixture over the potatoes. Top with flakes of the remaining butter.

5 Bake in the centre of the oven for about 1 hour. If the top begins to turn too brown, cover with foil.

Variation: Another version of this famous dish is made without eggs, using single cream instead of milk. To serve the gratin as a light main meal, sprinkle with plenty of grated cheese, such as Gruyère, 10 minutes before the end of cooking. Serve with a salad.

Note: In France, *Gratin dauphinois* is often served with fried or grilled meat. Since washing potatoes removes some of the starch needed for this dish, many people only wipe them clean.

Œufs en cocotte

Not difficult • Loire Valley

Egg ramekins

Serves 6

1 thick slice prosciutto or lean, unsmoked bacon (about 50 g)
50 g mushrooms
2 shallots
80 g butter
salt
freshly ground black pepper
½ tsp Dijon mustard
4 tbsp dry white Burgundy
3 to 4 sprigs tarragon
3 to 4 sprigs chervil
4 tbsp crème fraîche
6 fresh eggs

Preparation time: 30 minutes

1,400 kJ/300 calories per portion

1 Finely dice the prosciutto or bacon. Trim and wash the mushrooms, peel the shallots and chop both finely.

2 Melt 50 g of butter in a saucepan. Add the prosciutto or ham and the mushrooms and sauté for 2 to 3 minutes. Add the shallots and sauté for a further 4 to 5 minutes over low heat. Stir, and season with salt and pepper.

3 Add the mustard and wine and reduce the sauce until nearly all the liquid has evaporated. Meanwhile, wash the herbs, pat dry, chop finely and add to the sauce. Finally, add the crème fraîche and cook briefly.

4 Butter six ovenproof ramekins. Fill each ramekin a third of the way up with the mixture, and break an egg on top of each. Place the ramekins in a large bain-marie *(see Glossary)*. Cover and cook over medium heat for 8 to 10 minutes, until the egg whites are set but the yolks are still soft.

5 If you like, top with knobs of butter and garnish with chervil leaves. Serve at once.

Escargots aux fines herbes

Snails in herb sauce

More complex • Languedoc

Serves 4

2 onions
1 garlic clove
200 g prosciutto or lean, unsmoked bacon
100 g spinach
½ lettuce heart
½ endive
30 g parsley
75 g chervil
6 tbsp olive oil
2 tbsp flour
40 cl meat stock
4 dozen canned snails
4 tbsp wine vinegar
10 black peppercorns
1 bouquet garni
4 shelled walnuts
salt
freshly ground black pepper
2 egg yolks, beaten

Preparation time: 1¾ hours

2,400 kJ/570 calories per portion

1 Peel and finely chop the onions and garlic. Cut the prosciutto or bacon into small dice (*above*). Wash the spinach, salad greens and herbs. Pat dry and chop them all very finely.

2 Heat the olive oil in a saucepan and fry the onions and garlic until transparent. Stir in the prosciutto or bacon, then the salad greens and herbs. Sprinkle with the flour. Pour in the stock (*above*) and stir thoroughly. Cover the pan and leave to simmer over very low heat for about 1 hour.

3 Meanwhile rinse the snails thoroughly under cold running water and drain. Place some water in a saucepan, and add the wine vinegar, peppercorns and bouquet garni. Simmer the snails in the water for about 15 minutes. Drain through a colander and leave to cool.

4 When the sauce has thickened, add the snails and allow to stand for 10 to 15 minutes. Finely chop the walnuts and add to the sauce. Taste and season with salt and pepper. Finally, bind with the egg yolks (*above*). Serve with fresh white bread. If you like, garnish with some sprigs of rosemary.

Wine: One of the light Languedoc reds is a good choice.

Note: Snails were a prized food as far back as Roman times, when they were fattened in special gardens. Today, the most popular snails in France are those from vineyards, especially in Burgundy and Languedoc.

Preparing fresh snails is a complex and time-consuming process, as they have to be allowed to fast for some days to clean impurities from their system. It is easier to buy them ready prepared, either canned or frozen.

Croûtes aux morilles

Morels in cream sauce

Simple but delicious • Franche-Comté

Serves 6 to 8

500 g fresh, or 50 g dried, morels
25 cl milk (if using dried morels)
100 g butter
10 cl meat stock
salt

For the béchamel sauce:
1 tbsp butter • 2 tbsp flour
10 cl cream
10 cl milk (if using fresh morels)
salt • freshly ground black pepper
grated nutmeg

12 to 16 slices white French bread

Preparation time: 45 minutes
(plus 2 to 3 hours soaking time)

1,300 kJ/310 calories per portion
(if serving 8)

1 If you are using dried morels, soak them in the milk, diluted with a little water, for 2 to 3 hours. Rinse under cold running water, then drain. Strain the milk through a fine sieve and reserve 10 cl. Fresh morels should be rinsed thoroughly in cold running water, because they often contain dirt.

2 Melt 70 g of the butter in a saucepan, and sauté the morels over low heat. Add the stock, season with salt and simmer for 15 to 20 minutes.

3 Meanwhile, make the sauce. In a small pan, melt the butter, sprinkle with the flour and cook, stirring, without letting the mixture brown. Stir in the cream and the milk (reserved milk, if using dried morels), and season with salt, pepper and nutmeg. Simmer, stirring, over low heat for about 10 minutes, until smooth and thickened.

4 Add the morels and stock to the sauce. Check for seasoning.

5 Fry the slices of bread in the remaining butter until golden. Pour the morel mixture into a deep serving dish and serve with the fried bread.

Wine: Yellow wine (*vin jaune*) from the Jura is particularly good with this dish.

Variation: Heat ready-made vol-au-vent cases in the oven, and fill with the mushroom and cream sauce.

Morels

Wild mushrooms have a special place in French cooking. Of the different varieties the most popular and valued are morels or *morilles*, also called sponge mushrooms because of their distinctive pitted and convoluted caps. Rivalling truffles in the intensity of their aroma—but not in their price—morels give a distinctive flavour to sauces or to stuffing for poultry.

Morels grow in sandy soil around forest edges and in clearings in elm, ash and fir forests; they flourish particularly in the woods of the French and Swiss Jura, where the prime locations are jealously guarded secrets. Not surprisingly, the best-known morel dishes originate from the mountainous region of Franche-Comté.

Fresh morels are available only during the brief season from late April to the end of May. Fortunately, they dry well and are available year-round in their preserved form. Dried morels themselves have long been considered a delicacy: the French King Louis XIII is said to have spent the hours before his death in 1643 preparing fresh morels for drying.

If fresh morels are used, they must be thoroughly washed, because the caps retain grit. Dried morels should be soaked in milk diluted with water. Fresh or dried, morels must always be cooked—they are toxic when raw.

Ratatouille

Provençal stewed vegetables

Not difficult • Provence

3 medium-sized aubergines
3 large ripe tomatoes
3 courgettes
3 sweet peppers
2 onions
10 cl olive oil
salt
freshly ground black pepper
2 garlic cloves
1 bouquet garni

Preparation time: 1½ hours

1,100 kJ/260 calories per portion

1 Peel the aubergines and cut them into 2 cm dice. Plunge the tomatoes in boiling water, skin and deseed them, and coarsely dice. Trim and wash the courgettes and cut into thick slices. Wash the peppers, remove the ribs and seeds, and cut into 1 cm-wide strips. Peel the onions and cut into fine rings.

2 Heat the olive oil in a heavy saucepan. Add the onions and sauté them briefly, until translucent. Add the aubergines, courgettes, sweet peppers and tomatoes and season with salt and pepper. Peel and crush the garlic and add to the pan together with the bouquet garni. Pour 1 to 2 cups cold water over the vegetables.

3 Cover the saucepan and bring to the boil, then cook slowly over very low heat for about 1 hour. Remove and discard the bouquet garni.

4 Serve warm as a starter with fresh, crusty white bread, or as an accompaniment to a main course.

Wine: A Provençal rosé is especially good with ratatouille.

Variation: Add 3 to 4 peeled and quartered new potatoes to the other vegetables. A fennel bulb, cut into strips, can also be added to give a distinctive flavour to the dish.

Note: Leftover ratatouille is also very good served cold as a snack.

Gratin de courge

Marrow gratin

Needs a little care • Provence

Serves 4

1 marrow (about 1.5 kg)
120 g butter
½ litre milk
2 tbsp flour
grated nutmeg
salt
freshly ground black pepper
4 eggs
2 tbsp fresh breadcrumbs

Preparation time: 1½ hours

2,400 kJ/570 calories per portion

1 Peel the marrow, remove the seeds and cut into dice. Melt 70 g of the butter in a saucepan, add the diced marrow and sauté over medium heat, stirring constantly, until all liquid has evaporated and the marrow is soft. Rub it through a sieve into a bowl, or purée in a food processor. Preheat the oven to 180°C (350°F or Mark 4).

2 Place the milk in a saucepan and bring to the boil. Meanwhile, melt 30 g of the remaining butter in another pan. Sprinkle with the flour and cook, stirring, without allowing the mixture to brown. Add the hot milk, stirring

briskly, and continue to cook and stir until the sauce is smooth and thickened. Season with nutmeg, salt and pepper, and remove from the heat.

3 Beat the eggs, mix with the puréed marrow and stir in the béchamel sauce. Adjust the seasoning if necessary.

4 Grease a baking dish with butter. Add the marrow mixture. Sprinkle the breadcrumbs on top. Melt the remaining butter and pour over the top.

5 Bake in the centre of the oven for about 30 minutes. Serve hot.

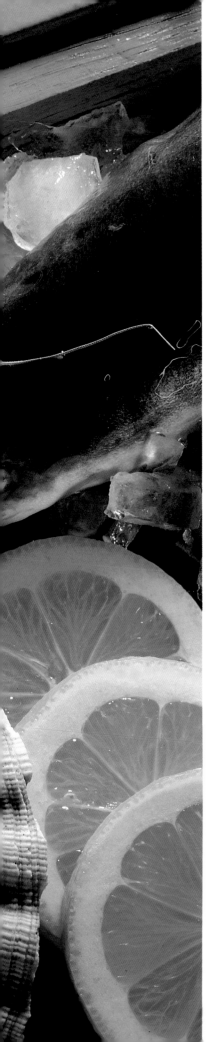

FISH AND SHELLFISH

With its long sea coast and many lakes and rivers, France is blessed with a wonderful variety of fish and shellfish: from the prized lobsters and oysters of the North Atlantic, to the pike and trout of the alpine lakes, to the sardines and squid from the sunny waters of the Mediterranean. Pollution of the country's inland waterways has taken its toll and the abundance of fish has dwindled. As a consequence of this decline, freshwater fish for the table is increasingly farm-bred. But these fish serve well in the many beguiling recipes developed over the years by a food-loving people.

Traditionally, the place of fish and seafood on a large, formal French menu is after the hot hors-d'œuvre and before the main meat course. However, depending on how it is prepared, a fish course can replace the soup, or the hot or cold hors-d'œuvre, or it can be served as the main course.

Chilled, dry white wine is usually the best choice to accompany simply prepared fish and shellfish, although in Normandy and Brittany the local dry cider is a popular alternative. With richly flavoured oily fish, such as salmon or mackerel, a young, light rosé is equally good. The French also drink red wine with fish, particularly if it has been used in the preparation of the dish.

Coquilles Saint-Jacques

Not difficult • Bordeaux **Scallops in cream sauce** *Serves 4*

12 scallops, cleaned, with corals
1 shallot
30 g parsley
3 tbsp oil
30 g butter
8 tbsp dry white wine
juice of ½ lemon
5 tbsp crème fraîche
salt
freshly ground black pepper

Preparation time: 20 minutes

960 kJ/230 calories per portion

1 Rinse the scallops under running water and pat dry. Separate the white flesh and the pink coral; dice the flesh coarsely, leaving the corals whole.

2 Peel the shallot and chop it into small pieces. Wash the parsley, pat dry and chop finely.

3 Heat the oil and butter in a shallow pan over low heat. Add the chopped shallot and the parsley and sauté briefly. Add the diced scallops and corals and cook for 1 to 2 minutes, stirring constantly. Remove from the oil with a slotted spoon and arrange on a warmed serving dish or individual shells (*see Note*). Keep warm.

4 Increase the heat to medium, and pour the wine and lemon juice into the pan, then stir in the crème fraîche. Season with salt and pepper and briefly bring to the boil, stirring constantly. Pour over the scallops and serve immediately, with fresh crusty bread.

Wine: This dish is good with a Muscadet or a white Gaillac.

Note: When buying fresh scallops— usually sold ready-opened and cleaned, attached to the flat half-shell—ask for the rounded top shells, which make attractive serving containers. To clean them, scrub vigorously with a nailbrush under cold running water.

Civet de langouste

Crawfish in red wine

Needs care • Languedoc

1 frozen crawfish, or spiny lobster,
tail (about 650 g), thawed
6 onions
2 shallots
1 garlic clove
50 g butter
5 cl brandy
½ litre dry red wine
1 bouquet garni
salt
freshly ground black pepper
1 tbsp flour

Preparation time: 1 hour

2,000 kJ/480 calories per portion

1 Cut the crawfish tail crosswise into segments, following the sections of the tail.

2 Peel and finely chop the onions, shallots and garlic, keeping each ingredient in a separate bowl.

3 Melt 30 g butter in a deep pan. Add the onions and sauté until transparent. Stir in the pieces of crawfish. Gently heat the brandy in a small pan, pour it over the crawfish and set it alight. Let the flames diminish, then carefully extinguish them by pouring in the red wine. Add the shallots, garlic and bouquet garni, and season with salt and pepper. Cover the pot and simmer over low heat for 5 to 8 minutes.

4 Remove the pieces of crawfish from the sauce and transfer them to a serving dish; keep warm. Remove and discard the bouquet garni.

5 Moisten the flour with some of the cooking liquid, then stir into the sauce. Simmer for 5 minutes. Stir in the remaining butter. Strain the sauce over the crawfish and serve immediately.

Wine: Serve this rich dish with a robust dry wine, such as a red or white Côtes du Roussillon.

Gratin de queues d'écrevisses

Crayfish gratin

Serves 6

1.5 kg live crayfish
about 1 litre vegetable stock, or
water
40 g butter
4 tbsp flour
4 cl dry vermouth
15 cl double cream
salt
freshly ground black pepper
2 tbsp grated, mild hard cheese

Preparation time: 1½ hours

1,800 kJ/430 calories per portion

1 Bring the stock or water to the boil in a large pan and drop in the crayfish. Boil vigorously for 8 to 10 minutes. Allow to cool, then remove them from the pan, reserving 40 cl of the stock. Peel the crayfish, cracking the claws to extract the flesh, and discard the shells. Remove the dark, vein-like intestines that run down the underside of each tail.

2 Preheat the oven to 220°C (425°F or Mark 7). Melt the butter in a saucepan over medium heat. Add the flour and whisk to make a roux. Add the reserved stock and the vermouth, bring to the boil and cook for 10 minutes to reduce. Add the cream and cook for a further 8 minutes. Season with salt and pepper, stirring well.

3 Put the crayfish in an ovenproof dish—reserving, if you like, a few tails for garnish. Pour over the sauce and sprinkle with the cheese. Bake in the centre of the oven for about 15 minutes, until golden-brown. Garnish with the reserved tails, if using.

Note: If fresh crayfish are not available, crayfish frozen in water may be obtainable from good fishmongers.

Crayfish

These small, clawed, freshwater crustaceans resemble miniature lobsters, but they have a much finer flavour than their larger relatives. Very popular in France—where they are known as *écrevisses*—they are particularly associated with the elaborately garnished dishes that characterized the *grande cuisine* of the 19th century.

Crayfish were once abundant on the Continent, but were rendered almost extinct by disease in 1876. Although they can still be caught in some lakes and lowland streams, today most commercial supplies are farmed in ponds. France imports the majority of its crayfish from central Europe, and only in certain areas, such as Franche-Comté, can stocks of wild crayfish still be found.

Although crayfish can be difficult to obtain, they are theoretically available all year round. As with most seafood, it is generally advisable to choose live specimens and cook them yourself.

A delicious and versatile shellfish, crayfish can be prepared in many different ways; one of the most luxurious dishes is a dozen or so of these little red-clawed crustaceans served *à la nage*—"swimming"— in a hot flavoured liquid (*court-bouillon*). Although only the claw and tail flesh is eaten, the crushed shells make a good base for a stock or a soup, and are the principal flavouring ingredient in the famous pink Nantua sauce.

Bouillabaisse

Mediterranean fish stew

Takes time • Provence

Serves 4

1 kg mixed fresh, or frozen,
Mediterranean fish (for example,
monkfish, red mullet, whiting, John
Dory, wrasse or conger eel)
1 onion
2 beef tomatoes
4 garlic cloves
15 g parsley
4 tbsp olive oil
4 bay leaves
400 mg powdered saffron
salt
freshly ground black pepper
8 thin slices French baguette or
other crusty white bread

For the rouille:
1 thick slice dry bread
1 garlic clove
1 dried red chili pepper
20 cl olive oil

Preparation time: 1¼ hours

**4,000 kJ/950 calories per portion
(including rouille)**

1 Rinse the fish under cold running water. If necessary, scale and gut the fish (*above*), removing the heads and tails. Cut the larger fish into portions.

2 Peel the onion and chop into small pieces. Plunge the tomatoes in boiling water briefly, skin them and cut in half. Scrape out the seeds, then dice the flesh. Peel the garlic and crush the flesh. Wash and dry the parsley.

3 Heat the oil in a large saucepan and sauté the onion. Add the tomatoes and the crushed garlic, followed by the parsley, bay leaves and saffron. Season with salt and pepper. Simmer over low heat for about 10 minutes.

4 In a separate pan, bring 1 litre water to the boil. Place the whole, firm-fleshed fish on top of the vegetables and herbs in the first pan. Cook for 2 to 3 minutes, then add the soft-fleshed fish and pour in the boiling water. Boil fiercely over high heat for 5 to 10 minutes, until the fish is cooked and the olive oil has emulsified in the liquid.

5 Meanwhile, prepare the *rouille*. Soak the slice of bread in lukewarm water. Peel the garlic and crush the flesh with a pestle and mortar. Add

the whole chili pepper and crush (*see Note, below*). Squeeze out the bread and mix it to a paste with the garlic and pepper. Stirring continuously, trickle in the oil to make a smooth sauce.

6 Lightly toast the slices of bread under the grill or in a dry frying pan. Arrange them in a warmed soup tureen.

7 Using a slotted spoon, carefully remove the fish from the pan and arrange the pieces on a warmed serving dish. Pour the fish soup over the toasted bread slices in the tureen and serve immediately.

8 Each person should be provided with a soup bowl and a plate. Serve the fish first onto the plates, so that everyone can remove the bones and skin and transfer the fish to their bowl. Then ladle the soup with the bread slices over the fish in the bowls. Pass the *rouille* separately accompanied by plenty of fresh, crusty white bread.

Wine: Choose a dry white wine or a fresh Rosé de Provence.

Note: Chili peppers contain volatile oils that can irritate the skin and burn the eyes. Handle them with care and wash your hands after using them.

Filets de sole à la bretonne

Not difficult • Brittany **Sole in white wine** *Serves 4*

1 leek
1 celery heart
1 onion
1 shallot
3 tbsp butter
8 sole fillets
flour for coating
10 cl dry white wine
salt
freshly ground black pepper
10 cl double cream
30 g flat-leaf parsley

Preparation time: 1 hour

*1,400 kJ/330 calories
per portion*

1 Trim and discard the green parts of the leek; wash and thinly slice the remaining white part. Slice the celery heart. Peel the onion and the shallot and chop finely.

2 Preheat the oven to 200°C (400°F or Mark 6). Melt the butter in a pan. Add the vegetables and sauté over low heat, without browning, for about 10 minutes. Put the partly cooked vegetables in an ovenproof dish.

3 Wash the sole fillets and pat dry. Dip them in the flour, coat evenly and shake gently to remove any excess flour. Fold the fillets in half and arrange them on top of the bed of vegetables. Add the wine, and season with salt and pepper.

4 Cover the dish and bake in the centre of the oven for about 5 minutes.

5 Remove from the oven, pour over the cream and gently shake the dish so that it mixes in with the other ingredients. Return the dish to the oven and cook uncovered for a further 5 to 10 minutes, until lightly browned.

6 Meanwhile, wash the parsley, pat dry and chop finely. Sprinkle over the fish and serve immediately, accompanied by crusty white bread.

Wine: A dry white Muscadet from Brittany is an ideal accompaniment to this dish.

Lotte farcie

Stuffed monkfish

Fairly easy • Brittany

Serves 4

1 cleaned monkfish (about 1 kg)
salt
freshly ground black pepper
50 g dry white bread
¼ litre milk
30 g mixed herbs (chervil, parsley,
fennel)
grated nutmeg
30 g butter
1.5 kg fresh mussels
10 cl Muscadet, or other dry white
wine

Preparation time: 1½ hours

1,600 kJ/380 calories per portion

1 Rinse the fish under cold, running water and pat dry. Using a sharp knife, make an incision along the spine and partly cut and lift the flesh away from the bones on either side to form two pockets. Season with salt and pepper.

2 Soak the bread in the milk, squeeze out and crumble into a bowl. Wash the herbs, pat dry and chop finely. Knead them into the moist bread. Season with nutmeg and plenty of salt and pepper. Divide the mixture in half, and spoon into the two pockets in the fish.

3 Preheat the oven to 200°C (400°F or Mark 6). Butter a shallow ovenproof dish. Place the fish in the dish.

4 Scrape, wash and beard the mussels. Tap sharply any that are open and discard any that do not close. Bring ¼ litre water to the boil in a pan, add the mussels, cover and cook over high heat until the shells open. Discard any that remain closed. Remove the mussels from the pan, shell them and set aside.

5 Strain the mussel liquor over the fish. Pour in the wine, and dot the fish with slivers of butter. Cook in the centre of the oven for 30 to 35 minutes, basting occasionally.

6 About 3 minutes from the end of the cooking time, arrange the mussels around the fish, return to the oven and heat through. Serve hot straight from the dish.

Sardines farcies aux épinards

Sardines stuffed with spinach

Takes time • Provence

Serves 4

500 g fresh sardines
300 g fresh spinach
salt
1 onion
10 cl milk
5 tbsp olive oil
1 tbsp flour
grated nutmeg
freshly ground black pepper
2 garlic cloves
2 tsp fresh breadcrumbs

Preparation time: 1¼ hours

1,300 kj/310 calories per portion

1 If necessary, gut and scale the sardines, removing the heads but not the tails, and rinse under cold running water. Open the sardines out, and with a sharp knife carefully prise the ribs and backbones away from the flesh (*above*). Lay them flat on a cloth.

2 Trim and thoroughly wash the spinach. Bring a pan of salted water to the boil and blanch the spinach for 1 to 2 minutes. Drain, squeeze out the excess moisture and chop finely (*above*). Peel and finely chop the onion.

3 Preheat the oven to 250°C (475°F or Mark 9). In a small saucepan, gently heat the milk. In another pan, heat 2 tbsp of the olive oil and sauté the onion until transparent. Add the spinach and sauté for a few minutes, stirring constantly. Stir in the flour, then the hot milk. Season with grated nutmeg,

salt and pepper. The mixture should be like a thickish sauce—add a little more flour if necessary. Simmer for 15 to 20 minutes over medium heat. Peel the garlic, crush the flesh and stir into the mixture. Remove from the heat.

4 Spread each sardine with 1 tsp of the spinach stuffing (*above*).

5 Grease the bottom of a shallow ovenproof dish with a little of the olive oil. Line the dish with the remaining spinach mixture. Roll up the sardines, starting at the head and working towards the tail, and arrange them in rows on the bed of spinach. Sprinkle with a thin layer of breadcrumbs and trickle the rest of the oil over the top.

6 Bake in the centre of the oven for about 15 minutes. Serve straight from the baking dish, with fresh bread.

Wine: This dish is good with a light Rosé de Provence or Tavel.

Note: The quantities given here are for a starter-size course; for a main course you should double the quantities.

Truites Mont-Dore

Trout in vermouth

Simple • Auvergne

Serves 4

4 cleaned trout
20 cl dry vermouth
salt
freshly ground black pepper
10 cl double cream
2 egg yolks
*80 g grated, mild hard cheese, such
as Gruyère*

Preparation time: 45 minutes

1,800 kJ/430 calories per portion

1 Preheat the oven to 180°C (350°F or Mark 4).

2 Rinse the trout carefully under cold running water and pat dry. Butter a shallow ovenproof dish, lay the trout in the dish and pour over the vermouth. Season with salt and pepper.

3 Place the dish in the centre of the oven and bake the trout for 15 to 20 minutes, according to size. Remove from the oven and increase the temperature to 250°C (475°F or Mark 9).

4 Whisk the cream and the egg yolks together in a bowl. Whisk in the juices from the fish. Pour the creamy sauce over the fish and sprinkle with the grated cheese.

5 Return the dish to the centre of the oven and bake for 3 to 4 minutes until lightly browned. Serve immediately.

Wine: A strong, full-flavoured white wine, such as Chablis or Vouvray, is an excellent accompaniment to this dish.

Trout

Native to the northern hemisphere, but now widely introduced to other areas, the trout belongs to the family of game and table fishes known as *Salmonidae*, of which the best known member is the salmon. The majority of trout species live in fresh water, although a few, such as the salmon—or sea—trout, migrate to the sea between spawnings.

One of the most prized varieties is the brown trout, which inhabits faster-running streams and rivers. A favourite of angler and gourmet alike, this red-speckled fish has a flavour superior to its more familiar lake-dwelling relative the black-spotted rainbow trout with its characteristic red stripe. Originally from North America, the rainbow trout is the trout species most readily available commercially; however, the majority on sale today have been artificially reared on fish farms, common in France and throughout Europe.

The most delicious way to serve fresh trout is absolutely plain; when buying fresh fish, look for specimens with glossy, firm flesh and clear, bright eyes. All fish require relatively brief cooking. To check for doneness, cut into the flesh at the thickest part; when the flesh is opaque and no longer clings to the bone it is done.

Brochet à la crème

Fairly easy • Auvergne   **Pike in cream sauce**   *Serves 6*

6 shallots
30 g parsley
150 g button mushrooms
50 g butter
1 cleaned pike (about 1.5 kg)
salt
freshly ground black pepper
75 cl dry white wine
25 cl crème fraîche
1 tbsp flour

Preparation time: 1½ hours

2,200 kJ/520 calories per portion

1 Peel and finely chop the shallots. Wash the parsley, pat dry and chop finely. Clean the mushrooms and trim off the base of the stalks. Rinse briefly under cold running water, then slice thinly. Mix the shallots, parsley and mushrooms together in a bowl.

2 Preheat the oven to 200°C (400°F or Mark 6). Generously butter a large roasting pan and put in the herb and mushroom mixture.

3 Wash the pike in cold water, pat dry and place in the pan on top of the mushroom mixture. Season with salt and pepper. Pour over about ¾ of the wine, so that the fish is half covered. Dot the fish with small flakes of butter.

4 Cut a sheet of greaseproof paper large enough to cover the fish. Melt the remainder of the butter and brush it over the paper. Lay the paper butter-side down on top of the fish (*above*). Place in the centre of the oven and cook for 30 to 35 minutes. Remove the fish and turn off the oven.

5 Transfer the fish to a warmed serving dish. With a knife, carefully remove the skin (*above*). Remove the mushroom mixture from the pan with a slotted spoon and arrange round the fish. Put the dish in the oven to keep the fish warm.

6 Pour the fish juices into a saucepan and bring to the boil. Add the crème fraîche and whisk. Mix the flour with a little water and whisk it into the sauce. Adjust the seasoning, adding more wine if necessary, and simmer for about 5 minutes. Pour the sauce over the fish, and serve immediately.

Wine: A dry white Burgundy, such as a Mâcon blanc, goes well with this dish.

Note: The firm, white flesh of the pike is very popular in central European cuisine. These predatory, freshwater fish can grow to 2 metres in length and weigh as much as 35 kg. However, it is young pike weighing between 1.5 and 2 kg that are most suitable for cooking.

Daube d'anguilles

Not difficult • Provence **Baked eel** *Serves 4*

4 leeks
4 garlic cloves
30 g parsley
1 bay leaf
salt
freshly ground black pepper
12 black olives, stoned
20 cl dry white wine
1 kg eel, skinned and cleaned
2 tbsp dry breadcrumbs
4 tbsp olive oil

Preparation time: 1 hour

3,800 kJ/900 calories per portion

1 Preheat the oven to 180°C (350°F or Mark 4). Trim and wash the leeks, discarding the green part. Thinly slice the white part and lay the slices in a shallow ovenproof dish. Peel and chop the garlic. Wash, pat dry and chop the parsley. Sprinkle the garlic and the parsley over the leeks and add the bay leaf. Season with salt and pepper. Scatter the olives over the bed of vegetables and pour in the wine.

2 Wash the eel under cold running water, pat dry and cut crosswise into portions. Arrange the pieces on top of the vegetables, sprinkle breadcrumbs over the top and dribble over the oil.

3 Cover, and bake in the centre of the oven for about 30 minutes (depending on the thickness of the eel). Serve straight from the dish.

Wine: Serve a red wine from the southern Côtes du Rhône, such as a Gigondas, or a light Provençal red.

Note: In Martigues, a fishing port near Marseille, this dish is traditionally served as part of the celebratory supper that precedes Midnight Mass on Christmas Eve.

Saumon aux échalotes

Salmon with shallots

Fairly easy • Loire Valley

Serves 4

1 kg piece fresh salmon
125 g rindless streaky bacon
150 g shallots
100 g butter
salt
freshly ground black pepper
3 tbsp good wine vinegar
1 tbsp flour

Preparation time: 1 hour

2,900 kJ/690 calories per portion

1 Preheat the oven to 220°C (425°F or Mark 7). Wash the salmon and pat dry. Remove the skin. Cut the bacon into thin strips about 4 cm long. With a sharp knife, pierce the flesh on the upper side of the salmon at intervals of 2 to 3 cm and insert the bacon strips.

2 Peel the shallots and chop finely. Line a shallow ovenproof dish with the shallots and lay the salmon on top. Cut 80 g of the butter into thin slivers and dot them on top of the salmon. Season with salt and pepper.

3 Cover the dish and bake the fish in the centre of the oven for 15 to 20 minutes. Reduce the oven temperature to 180°C (350°F or Mark 4). Pour the wine vinegar over the salmon and cook for a further 15 minutes, basting from time to time.

4 Meanwhile, blend the flour and the remaining butter and shape into little balls. Transfer the salmon to a serving dish. Add the flour balls to the juices and whisk in. Pour over the salmon and serve immediately, with crusty bread.

Wine: Choose a full-bodied white wine from the Loire to accompany this dish.

83

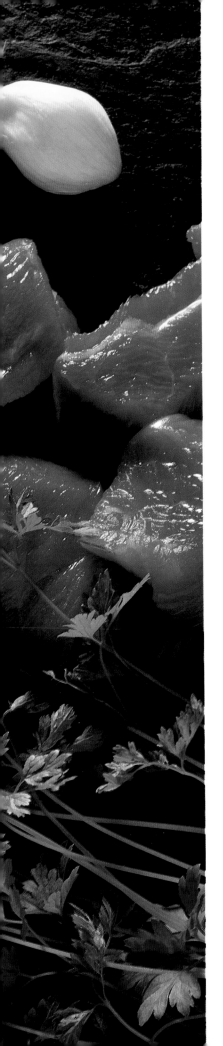

MEAT AND OFFAL

T he meat course is only one of the many episodes in the traditional French menu. It lends itself to a range of dishes of very diverse character.

Expensive, lean cuts of beef, lamb and veal are readily available, and can be cooked deliciously in a matter of minutes with a minimum of fuss. But the French are also renowned for their use of cheaper cuts—such as breast or shoulder of veal, pig's trotters or calf's head—which are presented with as much flair as more luxurious joints.

Offal, too, is popular, and has inspired many classic dishes, such as the famous *Tripe à la mode de Caen*. Fresh pork does not occupy a prominent place in traditional French *haute cuisine*, but smoked or salted it is the basis of many popular regional dishes, such as the boiled pork and vegetable *Potée bourguignonne*.

A mainstay of both provincial and *grande* cuisine are the many slowly cooked, one-pot stews. There are numerous examples, from the sturdy *cassoulet*, a casserole of meats and white beans, to the aromatic *daube*, with its rich wine marinade. Each region has its own specialities.

Red meat dishes, such as roast lamb or beef, or a hearty casserole, are generally best accompanied by a full-bodied red wine. With veal or pork, a lighter red, a rosé or a dry white may be preferable.

Potée bourguignonne

Not difficult • Burgundy **Pork pot**

500 g salt pork shoulder
1 salt pork knuckle
500 g rindless smoked streaky bacon
1 small white cabbage
6 carrots
4 small white turnips
4 kohlrabi
6 leeks
1 onion
2 garlic cloves
5 cloves
freshly ground white pepper
salt
500 g waxy potatoes

For the mustard sauce:
50 g butter
50 g flour
1 litre meat stock
5 tbsp Dijon mustard
1 tbsp wine vinegar
3 tbsp crème fraîche
salt
freshly ground black pepper
4 egg yolks

Preparation time: 2½ hours
(plus 12 hours soaking time)

3,700 kJ/880 calories per portion

1 Soak the salt meat in plenty of fresh water for up to 12 hours, or overnight, changing the water occasionally.

2 Place the meat and the bacon in a large, heavy cooking pot. Pour in enough cold water to cover the meat and bring to the boil. Reduce the heat to low and simmer gently for about 2 hours, skimming off surface froth as it forms.

3 While the meat is simmering, trim and core the cabbage and cut into quarters. Peel the carrots and cut into quarters. Add the cabbage and carrots to the pot. Trim and peel the turnips and the kohlrabi. Trim the leeks, retaining only the white part, and wash thoroughly. Cut all three vegetables into halves or quarters, depending on their size, and add them to the pot.

4 Peel the onion and the garlic and leave whole. Spike the onion with the cloves, and add it to the pot together with the garlic. Season with pepper, and salt if necessary.

5 About 30 minutes before the meat is done, peel the potatoes, cut them into halves or quarters, depending on their size, and add them to the pot. Continue cooking until everything is tender.

6 Meanwhile, prepare the sauce: melt the butter in a saucepan over low heat, mix in the flour with a wooden spoon and cook, stirring, for about 2 minutes. Add the meat stock and, whisking continuously, cook it until it is smooth and comes to the boil. Stir in the mustard, wine vinegar and crème fraîche. Season with salt and pepper and remove the pan from the heat.

7 Beat the egg yolks in a bowl and stir gradually into the sauce, continuing to whisk until it thickens. If necessary, return the pan to the heat briefly but do not let it boil. Adjust the seasoning.

8 Remove the meat from the pot. Carve it and arrange the slices on a warmed serving dish. Discard any vegetables that have lost their shape, and arrange the rest round the meat. Serve the mustard sauce separately. The cooking liquid can be strained and served on its own as a broth to precede the main course; alternatively it can be reserved as a base for a soup or stew.

Wine: A light red Burgundy, such as a Mâcon, goes well with this dish.

Variation: Raw garlic sausage or salt neck of pork can also be added to this dish. White haricot beans are another traditional accompaniment to salt pork; if using, soak in cold water for about 6 hours beforehand, and add directly to the pot with the meat.

If salt pork is difficult to obtain, you can use raw, smoked loin of pork; this does not need soaking.

Note: *Potée,* which traditionally includes salt pork and cabbage, is a typical French farmhouse recipe.

Choucroute garnie

Garnished sauerkraut

1 kg raw sauerkraut
1 large onion
30 g goose fat or lard
5 juniper berries
1 bay leaf
salt
freshly ground black pepper
¼ litre dry white wine
500 g thick rashers smoked streaky bacon, rinds removed
8 medium-sized waxy potatoes
4 raw smoked pork loin chops
8 small frankfurters
1 tbsp kirsch
1 garlic clove

Preparation time: 2¾ hours

7,800 kJ/1,900 calories per portion

1 Wash the sauerkraut and squeeze out the excess moisture. Peel and chop the onion.

2 In a large fireproof casserole or heavy pan, melt the goose fat or lard over low heat. Put half the sauerkraut in the pot. Add the chopped onion, juniper berries and the bay leaf. Season with salt and pepper. Place the rest of the sauerkraut in a loose layer on top. Pour in the wine and an equal quantity of water. Bring the liquid to a low simmer, then cover and simmer over low heat for 1 hour. If the sauerkraut becomes too dry, add a little water.

3 Lay the bacon rashers on top of the sauerkraut and replace the lid. Continue to cook for about 30 minutes.

4 Peel and halve the potatoes and embed them in the sauerkraut. Cook for a further 30 minutes.

5 Add the chops to the pot and simmer for another 10 minutes. Then add the frankfurters and cook for a further 10 minutes, or until heated.

6 Remove the pan from the heat and stir in the kirsch. Peel and crush the garlic and mix it into the sauerkraut. If necessary, adjust the seasoning. Arrange the ingredients on a warmed serving dish and serve immediately.

Drink: A full-bodied Alsace Riesling or beer goes well with this dish.

Escalopes aux pruneaux

Fairly easy • Loire Valley **Pork escalopes with prunes** *Serves 4*

250 g stoned prunes
¼ litre medium-dry white wine (for example, Vouvray)
4 pork escalopes, about 1 cm thick
salt
freshly ground black pepper
plain flour
30 g butter, or 2 to 3 tbsp oil
1 tbsp tomato purée
3 tbsp crème fraîche

Preparation time: 40 minutes (plus 3 to 4 hours soaking time)

1,400 kJ/330 calories per portion

1 Marinate the prunes in the wine in a covered bowl for 3 to 4 hours.

2 Put the prunes and wine into a saucepan and cook, covered, for about 20 minutes. Meanwhile, rinse the escalopes under cold running water and pat dry. Season with salt and pepper and coat with flour, tapping the meat to remove any excess.

3 Melt the butter in a deep frying pan and fry the escalopes over medium heat for about 3 minutes on each side.

4 Remove the escalopes from the pan and place them on a warmed serving dish. Strain the wine from the prunes into the pan containing the meat juices. Arrange the prunes around the meat and keep warm.

5 Increase the heat and boil the pan juices until reduced by half. Reduce the heat, stir in the tomato purée and the crème fraîche and heat gently. Pour the sauce over the escalopes. Serve with rice.

Wine: A light, dry red Loire wine from the Touraine goes well with this dish.

Note: Vouvray is a wine from the Touraine, best-known in its sparkling version. Any of the many medium-dry white wines from the Loire Valley are suitable for this dish.

Tripes à la mode de Caen

More complex • Normandy

Tripe in cider and calvados

Serves 6

1 kg cooked tripe
2 calf's feet (ask your butcher to cut
them into slices)
pork rind for lining the pot (about
125 g)
2 carrots
4 onions
1 leek
2 garlic cloves
4 cloves
1 bouquet garni
salt
freshly ground black pepper
35 to 40 cl dry cider
1½ tbsp calvados

Preparation time: 2¾ hours

2,300 kJ/550 calories per portion

1 Wash the tripe thoroughly under cold running water. Place it on a chopping board and, using a very sharp knife, cut it into strips about 2 cm wide (*above*). Wash the calf's feet slices.

2 Remove the meat from the calf's feet and cut it into small pieces (*above*), reserving the bones. Blanch the pork rind in boiling water.

3 Peel, wash and slice the carrots. Peel the onions and cut into quarters. Trim the leek, discarding the dark green part, and wash thoroughly. Peel and coarsely chop the garlic.

4 Line a cast-iron or other fireproof casserole with the pork rind. Place the reserved bones, the vegetables, garlic, cloves and bouquet garni in the pot and season with salt and pepper. Lay the tripe and the meat from the calf's feet on top. Pour over enough cider to cover the tripe. Add the calvados and season again with salt and pepper.

5 Tightly cover the pot. If you do not have one with a hollowed-out lid (*below*), use a shallow, heatproof dish

for a lid. Fill the lid with ice cubes or cold water and cook the tripe over very low heat for at least 2 hours, topping up the water or ice cubes as necessary.

6 When the tripe is tender, remove the bones, leek and the bouquet garni from the liquid and discard them. Skim off the surface fat with a spoon, or with ice cubes wrapped in kitchen paper wiped over the surface.

7 Serve the tripe very hot, with fresh white bread.

Drink: Accompany with generous quantities of dry cider, preferably from Normandy.

Note: Tripe is usually sold cleaned, washed and blanched. Lining the pot with pork rind prevents the tripe from sticking to the bottom. After 2 hours' cooking, the tripe will be tender but still firm; longer cooking—anything up to 20 hours for ox tripe—enables the flavours of the vegetables and seasoning to saturate the tripe without its disintegrating, and releases the natural gelatine from the calf's feet and pork rind to give the dish more body.

Entrecôte à la bordelaise

Not difficult • Bordeaux   **Entrecôte with red wine sauce**   *Serves 4*

800 g entrecôte, or sirloin, steak
1 tbsp olive oil
2 shallots
2 or 3 marrow bones
15 or 30 g butter (or 1 or 2 tbsp oil)
1 tbsp flour
20 cl red Bordeaux wine
salt
freshly ground black pepper

Preparation time: 1 hour
(plus 1 hour standing time)

2,400 kJ/570 calories per portion

1 With a sharp knife, score the sinews on the upper side of the steak so that it stays flat during grilling. Rub with the olive oil and leave to stand for about 1 hour.

2 Meanwhile, peel the shallots and chop them finely. Simmer the marrow bones in water for a few minutes until the marrow slips out easily. Allow it to cool slightly, then dice coarsely.

3 Melt 15 g butter in a saucepan and sauté the shallots until transparent. Sprinkle with the flour, then add the wine. Season with salt and pepper and simmer for about 10 minutes. Add the diced bone marrow and simmer for a further 10 minutes.

4 Grill the steak—or fry it in 15 g butter in a heavy frying pan over high heat—until cooked to the desired degree of doneness, turning once. Season with salt and pepper.

5 Leave the meat to stand briefly, then cut into portions and transfer to a warmed serving dish. Pour over the sauce and serve immediately.

Wine: A good red Bordeaux, such as a Saint-Émilion, goes well with this dish.

Variations: Instead of the sauce, serve the entrecôte with herb butter. Pound finely chopped shallots and fresh mixed herbs into slightly softened butter—about 1 shallot and 30 g herbs to 150 g butter—then chill.

Steak du Morvan

Fillet steak in Chablis sauce

Serves 4

6 shallots
4 beef fillet steaks, about 2 cm thick
(about 200 g each)
30 g butter (or 2 tbsp oil)
salt
freshly ground black pepper
1 tsp Dijon mustard
10 cl Chablis

Preparation time: 25 minutes

1,800 kJ/430 calories per portion

1 Peel and finely chop the shallots. Rinse the meat under cold running water and pat dry.

2 Heat a heavy frying pan until very hot. Without adding fat, briefly sear the steaks on each side. Add 1 tbsp butter and let it run under the meat. Fry the steaks on each side over high heat to the desired doneness (about 6 minutes in all for medium-rare steak). Season with salt and pepper, remove from the pan and keep warm.

3 Add the remainder of the butter to the pan and sauté the shallots until transparent. Mix the mustard with the wine, then pour onto the shallots and stir with a wooden spoon. Season to taste and reduce the sauce a little. Pour the sauce over the steaks and serve immediately, accompanied by fresh crusty bread or French fries.

Wine: A fine red Bourgogne Premier Cru or a Beaujolais-Villages goes well with this dish.

Note: The appeal of this relatively simple dish lies in its high-quality ingredients. If you cannot get Chablis, use another good quality white Burgundy such as a Pouilly-Fuissé.

Bœuf en daube
Pot-roasted beef in red wine

750 g beef without bones (shin, leg or chuck)
pork rind for lining the pot (about 125 g)
200 g rindless smoked streaky bacon
60 g parsley
4 garlic cloves
6 shallots
salt
freshly ground black pepper
1 onion
3 cloves
1 sprig thyme
1 bay leaf
quatre épices (see Glossary)
35 to 40 cl full-bodied red wine (for example, Cahors or Châteauneuf-du-Pape)

Preparation time: 5½ hours

3,500 kJ/830 calories per portion

1 Rinse the meat under cold running water, pat it dry and cut it into large cubes. Blanch the pork rind in boiling water.

2 Finely dice the streaky bacon. Wash the parsley, pat dry, and chop finely. Peel and finely chop the garlic and the shallots. Mix the diced bacon, parsley, garlic and shallots together in a bowl.

3 Line a cast-iron (*see Step 5, below*), or other fireproof casserole with the pork rind. Layer half the beef across the bottom and season with salt and pepper. Sprinkle half the bacon and herbs mixture on top.

4 Add the rest of the beef, season, and top with the remaining bacon and herbs mixture. Peel the onion and spike it with the cloves. Add it to the pot together with the thyme, bay leaf and a little *quatre épices*. Pour over the red wine.

5 Tightly cover the casserole. A sheet of foil between the pot rim and the lid helps to prevent evaporation. Or use a hollowed-out lid, or shallow heatproof dish, filled with ice cubes or cold water (*see page 90, Step 5*). Cook over the lowest possible heat for about 5 hours. Do not lift the lid while cooking.

6 Before serving, skim off the surface fat (*above*) with a spoon—or with some ice cubes wrapped in kitchen paper wiped over the surface. Serve straight from the casserole, accompanied by plenty of fresh crusty bread.

Wine: Accompany the beef with a dark, strong red wine, preferably the same variety as that used in the preparation of the dish.

Note: Cooking meat *en daube* means to simmer it very slowly in a spicy sauce, usually one based on red wine; the name comes from that of the heavy pot traditionally used. Beef prepared in this way is often referred to simply as *daube*. Pork, lamb, chicken, rabbit, hare and pheasant can also be cooked *en daube*.

Escalopes de veau

Simple • Périgord

Veal escalopes in shallot sauce

Serves 4

4 veal escalopes (about 125 g each)
2 tbsp olive oil
3 to 4 shallots
½ tbsp lard
½ tbsp flour
30 cl meat stock
salt
freshly ground black pepper
1 stalk chervil
15 g flat-leaf parsley

Preparation time: 40 minutes

790 kJ/190 calories
per portion

1 Wash the escalopes and pat dry. Heat the oil in a frying pan and fry the escalopes over very high heat for 2 to 3 minutes on either side, until lightly browned. Remove from the pan and keep warm.

2 Peel and finely chop the shallots. Melt the lard into the cooking juices in the frying pan and sauté the shallots until light golden-brown. Sprinkle in the flour and stir with a wooden spoon until the flour is a light brown colour. Whisk in the stock and season with salt and pepper.

3 Cover the pan and simmer over low heat for about 10 minutes. Meanwhile, wash the chervil and the parsley. Pat dry, and chop finely.

4 Place the escalopes on a warmed serving dish. Pour over the sauce and sprinkle with the chopped chervil and parsley. Serve at once, accompanied by pasta or fresh crusty bread.

Wine: A light rosé from southern France goes well with this dish.

Note: Lard is widely used for cooking in the Périgord. If you prefer, you can use butter instead.

Ris de veau normand

Calf's sweetbreads with apples and calvados

Slightly more complex • Normandy

Serves 4

700 g calf's sweetbreads
salt
50 g butter
grated nutmeg
freshly ground black pepper
4 small, tart apples
2 tbsp calvados
15 cl double cream

Preparation time: 45 minutes
(plus 2 hours soaking time)

1,700 kJ/400 calories per portion

1 Soak the sweetbreads in water for about 2 hours.

2 Drain the sweetbreads. Put them in a saucepan and cover with cold water. Add salt, bring slowly to a gentle simmer and cook for 3 to 4 minutes.

3 Drain the sweetbreads and rinse them under cold running water. Remove the skin and carefully pat dry with kitchen paper.

4 Melt half the butter in a saucepan. Add the sweetbreads, and season with nutmeg and pepper, adding a little salt if necessary. Cover the pan and cook over medium heat for 8 to 10 minutes.

5 Meanwhile, cut the apples into quarters, core them, but leave the peel on. Melt the remaining butter in a pan and sauté the apples for about 10 minutes until soft. If necessary, moisten the apples with 1 tbsp water.

6 Transfer the cooked sweetbreads to a warmed serving dish. Warm the calvados in a ladle, set it alight and carefully pour it over the meat. Bind the remaining pan juices with the cream and reduce a little, if desired.

7 Arrange the apples pieces round the sweetbreads. Pour the sauce over the sweetbreads and serve.

Drink: Dry Normandy cider goes particularly well with this dish.

Note: Sweetbreads are a calf's thymus glands. Easy to digest, they are full of vitamins and very nourishing.

Blanquette de veau

Blanquette of veal

More complex • Île de France

Serves 4

1 kg boned shoulder of veal
1 to 2 veal bones
¼ litre dry white wine
salt
1 large onion
4 cloves
2 carrots
1 leek
1 garlic clove
1 bouquet garni
½ tsp black peppercorns
60 g butter
1 tbsp flour
8 large spring onions
250 g small button mushrooms
juice of 1 lemon
freshly ground black pepper
1 egg yolk
10 cl crème fraîche

Preparation time: 1¾ to 2¼ hours

3,400 kJ/810 calories per portion

1 Rinse the meat and bones under cold running water and pat dry. Cut the meat into large cubes and place them and the bones in a large fireproof casserole. Pour in the wine and top up with water so that the meat is covered. Season with salt. Bring to the boil and skim off any surface froth as it forms.

2 Meanwhile, peel the onion and spike it with the cloves. Peel and wash the carrots and cut them into quarters. Clean the leek, cut it in half lengthwise and wash thoroughly. Peel the garlic clove. Add the onion, carrots, leek, garlic, bouquet garni and peppercorns to the casserole. Cover and simmer over low heat for 1 to 1½ hours.

3 Meanwhile, make the roux. In a small saucepan, melt half the butter over low heat, add the flour and cook for about 2 minutes, stirring constantly, without allowing it to brown. Remove from the heat and leave to cool.

4 Trim and peel the spring onions. In another saucepan, melt 15 g butter. Add 1 tbsp veal stock from the pot and cook the spring onions whole, tossing occasionally, until the liquid evaporates. Do not allow the spring onions to brown.

5 Trim the mushrooms and wipe clean. Melt the remaining butter in another pan. Add the mushrooms, lemon juice, salt and pepper, and cook for about 10 minutes, stirring frequently.

6 When the meat is cooked, strain the stock into a saucepan. Pick out and discard the bones, vegetables and the bouquet garni. Return the meat to the casserole. Reserve 3 tbsp of the stock. Add the cooled roux to the remainder of the stock and, whisking constantly, simmer the sauce until it thickens slightly. If it seems too thin, add a little flour mixed with water.

7 Meanwhile, whisk the egg yolk with the crème fraîche. Stir in the reserved 3 tbsp veal stock, then mix it into the sauce.

8 Add the sauce, mushrooms and spring onions to the meat in the casserole and slowly heat through over low heat, without allowing it to boil. Serve straight from the casserole.

Wine: Serve a young Beaujolais or a dry white wine from the Loire with this dish.

Variations: Instead of using boned shoulder of veal and veal bones you can substitute 1.5 kg breast of veal, including bones; the meat should be cut into ribs before cooking. This recipe is also suitable for lamb or chicken.

Note: Blanquette is the general term for a ragout based on white meat—chicken, lamb, veal—plus mushrooms and spring onions, and a sauce made with a light-coloured roux.

Gigot à l'auvergnate

Roast leg of lamb

Not difficult • Auvergne

Serves 4

1 kg waxy potatoes
100 g soft butter
grated nutmeg
salt
freshly ground black pepper
150 g rindless green streaky bacon
1 leg of lamb (about 1 kg)
2 garlic cloves

Preparation time: 30 minutes
(plus 1½ to 2 hours cooking time)

5,000 kJ/1,200 calories per portion

1 Peel and finely slice the potatoes. Butter a roasting pan and line it with a thick layer of potato slices. Season with nutmeg, salt and pepper. Flake 60 g of the remaining butter over the potatoes. Dice the bacon and sprinkle it on top. Pour over about 20 cl water.

2 Preheat the oven to 250°C (475°F or Mark 9). Wash the lamb and pat dry. Melt the rest of the butter, without allowing it to brown, and brush it over the lamb. Peel the garlic cloves and cut them lengthwise into slivers. With the tip of a sharp knife, make 5 mm incisions at regular intervals in the upper side of the meat and insert the slivers of garlic.

3 Arrange the lamb on the bed of potatoes and season with salt and pepper. Roast, uncovered, in the centre of the oven for 1½ to 2 hours. Serve straight from the roasting pan, accompanied by green beans.

Wine: Serve with a good red Burgundy, such as Beaujolais-Villages.

Note: This dish traditionally calls for a leg of mutton; however, though less expensive than lamb, mutton is rarely available today. Most lamb sold comes from animals aged between 4 and 6 months old, when the meat is lean and tender. If the animal is more than a year old, the meat becomes mutton.

Tranches de gigot à la menthe

Lamb chops with fresh mint

Quick and easy • Lyonnais

Serves 4

4 gigot or lean chump chops (about 150 g each)
2 sprigs fresh mint
freshly ground black pepper
2 tbsp olive oil
salt
juice of 1 lemon

Preparation time: 20 minutes
(plus 4 hours marinating time)

1,700 kJ/400 calories per portion

1 Rinse the chops under cold, running water, dry thoroughly and put on a dish. Wash the mint, pat dry and scatter the leaves over the meat. Season with pepper and sprinkle with the olive oil. Leave to marinate for about 4 hours.

2 Preheat the grill.

3 Season the lamb steaks with salt and pepper and grill them for 3 to 4 minutes on each side.

4 Arrange the chops on a warmed serving dish and sprinkle them with the lemon juice. Serve immediately accompanied by green beans and fresh brown bread.

Wine: A red Bordeaux such as Médoc or Graves goes well with this dish.

Note: Gigot is the French name for a leg of lamb. Gigot chops, cut from the tender fillet end of the leg, are particularly good for grilling or frying. The quantities given above are enough for 4 people if a substantial starter is served beforehand. Otherwise, allow 2 steaks per person.

Côtes d'agneau persillées

Simple • Provence

Provençal-style lamb cutlets

Serves 4

8 double lamb cutlets (about 2 cm thick, 125 to 150 g each)
60 g parsley
6 tbsp fresh breadcrumbs
5 to 6 garlic cloves
salt
freshly ground black pepper
30 g butter
4 tbsp olive oil

Preparation time: 45 minutes

3,000 kJ/710 calories per portion

1 Preheat the oven to 250°C (475°F or Mark 9). Rinse the cutlets under cold running water and pat dry.

2 Wash the parsley, shake dry and chop finely. Mix the parsley with the breadcrumbs. Peel the garlic, crush the flesh and add it to the breadcrumb mixture. Season with salt and pepper.

3 Melt the butter in a frying pan and fry the cutlets for 2 to 3 minutes on each side. Arrange the cutlets in an ovenproof dish, season with salt and pepper, and coat them with a thick layer of the breadcrumb mixture. Sprinkle with the olive oil.

4 Bake in the centre of the oven for 8 to 10 minutes, until the breadcrumbs are crisp and lightly browned. Serve with grilled tomatoes or green beans.

Wine: A red Provençal wine, such as Côtes-de-Provence or Côtes-du-Rhône, goes well with this dish.

Côtes d'agneau normandes

Lamb cutlets with onion purée

Not difficult • Normandy

Serves 4

8 lamb cutlets (about 1.5 cm thick)
juice of 1 lemon
3 Spanish onions
70 g butter
salt
freshly ground black pepper
¼ litre meat stock
1 tbsp fresh breadcrumbs

*Preparation time: 45 minutes
(plus 1 hour standing time)*

3,700 kJ/880 calories per portion

1 Wash the cutlets under cold running water and pat dry. Sprinkle them with the lemon juice and leave to stand for about 1 hour.

2 Peel and coarsely chop the onions. Melt 20 g of the butter in a pan and sauté the onions over low heat without letting them brown. Season with salt and pepper. Add the stock and simmer for a further 30 minutes until very soft.

3 Meanwhile, melt 10 g of the butter and brush the cutlets with it. Season the cutlets with salt and pepper and coat with the breadcrumbs.

4 Heat the remaining butter in a frying pan and fry the cutlets for about 4 minutes on each side.

5 Transfer the onions to a bowl and mash them with a fork (or purée them in a food processor), then return the purée to the pan and reheat. Heap the purée on a warmed plate, arrange the cutlets on top, and serve with fresh crusty bread.

Drink: Serve with a red Loire wine, or, if you like, with dry cider.

Note: Lamb from the north of France is regarded as a particular delicacy; its distinctive salty taste derives from the salt meadows along the shores of the Atlantic on which the sheep graze.

POULTRY AND GAME

"**P**oultry," wrote the 19th-century French gastronome Brillat-Savarin, "is for the cook what canvas is to the painter." Guinea fowl, duck, goose and, above all, chicken offer the French cook a wide range of possibilities. The different birds can be flavoured and prepared in numerous ways: roasted or stewed, with or without sauce, whole or in pieces. Quick sautéing seals in flavour, a slow braise makes tough, older birds tender and succulent. The Bresse area near Burgundy is renowned for producing France's best chickens, but every region has its local recipes. As well as poultry, the French are fond of rabbits and quail, now farm-reared and widely available.

As for game, hunting has long been one of France's most popular pastimes. When the season opens in early autumn, fields and woods are crowded with eager sportsmen. Mountains and forests harbour deer, wild boar and hare; in the air, duck, pheasant and wood-pigeon are targets for the guns. French menus feature both furred and feathered game, often combining the rich taste of the meat with the sharp tang of fruit.

It is a popular fallacy that white wines are the logical choice for poultry: light, young reds go equally well with subtly flavoured dishes, and fuller bodied wines with spicier meat. The strong taste of game is best complemented by an equally strong, full-bodied red wine.

Coq au vin

Not difficult • Burgundy **Chicken in red wine** *Serves 4*

1 oven-ready chicken (about 1.5 kg)
100 g rindless smoked streaky
bacon
12 shallots or small onions
70 g butter
2 tbsp flour
½ litre red Burgundy wine
3 tbsp brandy
1 bouquet garni
grated nutmeg
salt
freshly ground black pepper
200 g small mushrooms

Preparation time: 1¼ hours

3,700 kJ/880 calories per portion

1 Rinse the chicken in cold water, pat dry and cut into serving pieces. Finely dice the bacon. Peel and finely chop the shallots or onions.

2 Heat 50 g of the butter in a large fireproof casserole. Add the shallots or onions and bacon and cook until the vegetables turn transparent, about 5 minutes. Remove and reserve.

3 Add the chicken to the casserole and fry over high heat until golden all over. Sprinkle with the flour, add the shallots or onions and bacon, and cook briefly, stirring constantly. Stir in the wine and brandy, add the bouquet garni and season with nutmeg, salt and pepper.

4 Cover, and simmer over low heat for about 40 minutes, or until the meat is tender.

5 Meanwhile, trim the mushrooms and wipe them clean. Heat the remaining butter in a pan and cook the mushrooms for 5 to 10 minutes until tender.

6 Remove the chicken from the sauce and keep warm. Increase the heat and reduce the sauce, if necessary. Discard the bouquet garni. Adjust the seasoning and add the mushrooms to the sauce.

7 Arrange the chicken on a warm serving dish, pour over the sauce and serve with crusty, white bread.

Wine: The best accompaniment for *Coq au vin* and the following variations is the wine used to make the sauce.

Variations: Coq au Riesling
(Chicken in Riesling)

Fry the chicken portions in butter. Add the bouquet garni, shallots and some salt and pepper with ½ litre Riesling wine. Cover, and cook gently for about 40 minutes. Fry the mushrooms separately in butter and add to the pan at the end. Whisk in 2 to 3 tbsp crème fraîche to thicken and heat through without boiling.

Coq au vin de pays
(Country-style chicken)

Instead of red Burgundy, use a simple *vin ordinaire* and add 2 tbsp tomato purée to the sauce as it cooks.

Note: The chicken used here is a young one. Traditionally, older birds are used for *Coq au vin*; however, they need a longer cooking time—depending on the age of the bird—and may also need to be topped up with more wine.

Poulet sauté aux lardons

Not difficult • Périgord

Chicken with bacon and tomatoes

Serves 4

1 young oven-ready chicken (about 1.5 kg)
150 g rindless smoked streaky bacon
1 onion
2 tomatoes
2 tbsp oil
salt
freshly ground black pepper
2 sprigs thyme

Preparation time: 1¼ hours

3,300 kJ/790 calories per portion

1 Rinse the chicken under cold running water, pat dry and cut into 8 to 10 serving portions.

2 Cut the bacon into narrow strips. Peel and finely chop the onion. Plunge the tomatoes into boiling water; skin, halve crosswise, deseed and chop into small pieces.

3 Heat the oil in a fireproof casserole or heavy pan and fry the bacon until crisp and brown. Remove with a slotted spoon, drain on kitchen paper and set aside.

4 Add the onion to the pot and sauté until transparent, about 5 minutes. Add the chicken and brown on all sides over high heat. Season with salt and pepper, and stir in the thyme and tomatoes.

5 Reduce the heat to low, cover the pot and continue to cook for about 30 minutes. Add a little water if the dish becomes too dry. Finally, return the bacon to the sauce and heat through. Serve with fresh crusty bread.

Wine: This dish is good with a rosé or a young, light red Bordeaux.

Poulet à l'oseille

Fairly easy • Normandy

Chicken with sorrel sauce

Serves 4

1 young oven-ready chicken (about 1.5 kg)
salt
freshly ground black pepper
200 g sorrel
50 g butter
¼ litre dry apple juice or cider
1 egg yolk
20 cl crème fraîche

Preparation time: 1¾ hours

3,600 kJ/860 calories per portion

1 Rinse the chicken under cold running water, pat dry and cut into serving portions. Sprinkle with salt and pepper. Tear the sorrel leaves from their stems. Wash the leaves, pat dry and chop finely.

2 Heat the butter in a fireproof casserole or heavy non-reactive pan and fry the chicken over high heat until golden on all sides. Add the sorrel, reduce the heat and cook for a few minutes more. Season with salt and pepper. Pour in the apple juice or cider, cover, and simmer over low heat for about 45 minutes, until the chicken is tender.

3 With a slotted spoon, remove the chicken from the pot, drain, arrange on a serving dish and keep warm.

4 In a bowl, whisk the egg yolk with the crème fraîche. Whisk in a few tablespoons of the cooking liquid. Add the mixture to the pot and heat the sauce, without letting it boil and whisking continuously, until smooth. Pour a little of this sauce over the chicken and serve the rest in a sauceboat. If you like, garnish the chicken with fresh sorrel.

Wine: Serve with a fresh young Beaujolais.

Note: Do not cook sorrel in an aluminium pan. The herb contains an acid that attacks the metal and creates toxic substances.

Poule au pot farcie

Pot-roasted stuffed chicken

Takes time • Béarn

Serves 4

250 g carrots
250 g small white turnips
2 leeks
1 ready-cleaned young boiling fowl,
with giblets (about 1.5 kg)
1 marrow bone and 2 or 3 veal bones
1 onion • 5 cloves
1 bouquet garni • salt
1 day-old bread roll
30 g parsley • 1 sprig tarragon
50 g rindless smoked streaky bacon
50 g prosciutto
1 shallot
freshly ground black pepper
1 garlic clove • 1 egg

Preparation time: 3½ hours

2,700 kJ/640 calories per portion

1 In a large cooking pot, bring 3 litres of water to the boil. Peel the carrots and turnips, wash and trim the leeks, and cut into pieces. Wash the giblets and the bones in cold water. Spike the onion with the cloves. Add these ingredients to the boiling water with the bouquet garni and some salt, and simmer for about 1 hour.

2 Meanwhile, soak the bread in warm water and squeeze dry. Wash the herbs, pat dry and finely chop. Chop the bacon and prosciutto. Peel the shallot and cut into small pieces. In a bowl, knead the chopped ingredients together with the bread. Season with salt and pepper. Peel the garlic and crush into the mixture, and stir in the egg to bind.

3 Rinse the chicken in cold water and pat dry. Fill with the stuffing, sew up the cavity and truss the bird with kitchen twine (*see Glossary*).

4 Put the chicken in the pot, cover and simmer over low heat for about 2 hours, until tender. Older birds may take a little longer.

5 Remove and drain the chicken. Discard the twine and place the bird on a warmed serving dish. With a slotted spoon, remove the vegetables from the pan and arrange round the chicken. Serve with gherkins and crusty bread.

Note: The drained liquid can be reserved and used for stock or soup.

Poultry

The domesticated chicken has a revered place in the French kitchen for its variety and versatility. It has long been an important ingredient in French cuisine. The French distinguish chickens by age, and prepare them in different ways.

The *poussin* and the slightly older *coquelet*, both sold as poussin here, are young chickens between 4 to 6 weeks old, weighing 250 to 600 g. They can be fried, grilled or roasted. *Poulet* usually denotes a roasting chicken up to 6 months old, weighing up to 1.5 kg; a younger *poulet*, or spring chicken, is very tender and can also be grilled or sautéed.

Poulardes are particularly plump young birds, specially fattened on natural feed for roasting. Nowadays, what is sold as a capon (*chapon*)—strictly a force-fed castrated cock—is more likely to be a *poularde*. A *poule*, or boiling fowl, is an older, laying hen that is tougher than a roasting chicken but full of flavour. It is best tenderized by poaching or braising.

Whatever the cooking method, test a whole bird for doneness by pricking the thickest part of the thigh with a skewer; if the juices run clear, the bird is done. Test chicken pieces by pressing with a finger; the flesh should be firm and springy.

Pintade aux morilles

Fairly easy • Périgord **Guinea fowl with morels** *Serves 4*

¼ *litre milk*
50 g *dried or* 250 g *fresh morels*
1 *oven-ready guinea fowl*
(about 1.2 kg)
50 g *Petit Suisse or Gervais cheese*
(or other soft, full-cream cheese)
salt
freshly ground black pepper
200 g *rashers rindless smoked*
bacon
2 tbsp *oil*
2 tbsp *brandy*
10 cl *crème fraîche*

Preparation time: 1 hour
(plus 2 to 3 hours soaking time)

4,000 kJ/950 calories
per portion

1 If using dried morels, pour the milk into a bowl with ¼ litre water, add the morels and soak for 2 to 3 hours. Drain, rinse in cold water and pat dry. If using fresh morels, trim and wash carefully to remove any grit.

2 Preheat the oven to 250°C (475°F or Mark 9). Rinse the guinea fowl in cold running water and pat dry. Season the cheese with salt and pepper and use to stuff the bird. Sew up the body cavity and truss the bird with kitchen twine (*see Glossary*).

3 Cook the bacon until lightly crisp in a non-stick frying pan or under the grill and use to line the base of a roasting pan. Add the guinea fowl and cook in the centre of the oven for 45 minutes, basting first with a little water and then with the meat juices.

4 Meanwhile, heat the oil in a heavy saucepan and sauté the morels over low heat for about 15 minutes. Season with salt and pepper.

5 Take the guinea fowl out of the oven. Remove the kitchen twine. In a ladle, warm the brandy over a flame. Carefully light it, pour over the bird, and flambé briefly. Transfer the guinea fowl to a serving dish and keep warm.

6 Remove the bacon from the roasting pan and discard. Skim any excess fat from the juices left in the pan. Set the pan over low heat, and stir the crème fraîche into the juices until the sauce is hot but not boiling. Transfer to a sauceboat. Arrange the morels round the guinea fowl on the dish and serve at once accompanied by the sauce.

Canard à la bigarade

Duck with orange sauce

More complex • Gascony

Serves 4

1 oven-ready duck (about 1.5 kg)
salt
freshly ground black pepper
1 kg unwaxed oranges
250 g sugar
10 cl white wine vinegar
4 tbsp Armagnac

Preparation time: 1¾ hours

5,200 kJ/1,200 calories per portion

1 Preheat the oven to 250°C (475°F or Mark 9). Wash the duck inside and out, and pat dry. Season with salt and pepper. Roast in a pan set in the middle of the oven for about 30 minutes, turning once, until crisp and brown.

2 Meanwhile, pare the outer zest (without white pith) from the oranges, and cut it into very fine strips, or *julienne*. Squeeze the oranges, reserve the juice and discard the flesh.

3 In a saucepan over medium heat, dissolve the sugar in the wine vinegar, stirring constantly with a wooden spoon until it caramelizes (*see Glossary)*; remove from the heat.

4 When the duck has browned, pour the juices into a second pan, skimming off surface fat, and reserve. Add a little of the orange juice to the roasting pan and pour the caramel over the duck, then sprinkle with the orange strips.

5 Reduce the oven temperature to 200°C (400°F or Mark 6). Roast the duck for about 1 hour more, until tender. Baste every 10 minutes with the pan juices, adding more orange juice, if necessary, for moistness.

6 Remove the duck from the oven, carve, arrange on a serving dish and keep warm. Stir the remaining orange juice into the reserved pan juices, heat through and transfer to a sauceboat. Gently warm the Armagnac in a ladle over a low flame, carefully pour over the duck and flambé briefly. Serve at once with fresh crusty bread and the sauce.

Wine: A good accompaniment is a light red Bordeaux Supérieur.

Note: Traditionally, this recipe specifies wild duck and bitter oranges.

Alicot

Takes time • Périgord · **Goose giblet stew**

300 g scorzonera (black salsify)
1 tsp lemon juice
300 g carrots
750 g ceps or other mushrooms
12 sweet chestnuts
1 kg goose giblets (gizzard, wing tips and neck—but not liver)
2 tbsp goose fat
1 bouquet garni
2 tbsp tomato purée
grated nutmeg
salt
freshly ground black pepper

Preparation time: 2¾ hours

4,500 kJ/1,100 calories per portion

1 Preheat the oven to maximum temperature. Scrape the scorzonera under cold running water, and cut into finger-length pieces. Bring water to boil in a non-reactive pan, add the lemon juice and blanch the scorzonera for 2 to 3 minutes. Peel and wash the carrots, cutting larger ones into finger-length pieces. Trim the mushrooms, wipe clean and chop finely.

2 With a sharp knife, make cross-shaped incisions in the chestnut shells. Place the chestnuts in a pan of boiling water for a couple of minutes to loosen the shells, then remove the shells and inner skin. Wash the giblets, pat dry and cut into bite-sized pieces.

3 Heat the goose fat in a frying pan. Sauté the mushrooms, remove from the pan, then fry the giblets briefly to brown them. Place the mushrooms, scorzonera, carrots and chestnuts in a fireproof casserole or heavy pan. Add the bouquet garni and tomato purée. Season with nutmeg, salt and pepper. Add 20 cl water and bring to the boil. Reduce the heat and add the giblets. Cover, and cook for about 2 hours over very low heat, or in a very low oven.

4 Discard the bouquet garni and serve with crusty brown bread.

Variation: The same dish can be made with duck or turkey giblets.

Pigeons rôtis

Fairly easy • the Landes · **Roast pigeon**

3 oven-ready pigeons, with livers and gizzards
salt
freshly ground black pepper
3 thin rashers unsmoked bacon
50 g goose fat
4 tbsp Armagnac
3 slices white bread
70 g butter

Preparation time: 45 minutes

2,400 kJ/570 calories per portion

1 Preheat the oven to 250°C (475°F or Mark 9). Wash the pigeons inside and out with cold water, pat dry and season with salt and pepper. Wrap them with the bacon rashers and truss with kitchen twine (*see Glossary*). Brush with a little of the goose fat.

2 Place the pigeons in a roasting pan and cook in the oven for 20 to 25 minutes.

3 Meanwhile, finely chop the gizzards and livers. In a frying pan, heat the remaining goose fat and cook the gizzards and livers for about 8 minutes, until soft. Lightly season with salt and pepper. Sprinkle with a little Armagnac and purée in a food processor.

4 Cut the bread slices in half diagonally. Melt the butter in a frying pan and fry the bread; spread with the puréed giblets and keep warm.

5 Remove the pigeons from the roasting pan. Discard the bacon and kitchen twine, cut the pigeons in half with kitchen shears, and keep warm. Set the pan over medium heat, and stir the rest of the Armagnac into the juices. Arrange the pigeons on a warmed serving dish with the bread. Serve the sauce separately. Green peas are an ideal accompaniment.

Wine: A red Graves goes particularly well with roast pigeon.

Lapin au vermouth

Rabbit with vermouth

Serves 4

*1 oven-ready rabbit (about 1.3 kg),
with liver*
30 cl dry vermouth
2 sprigs thyme
1 bay leaf
1 onion
6 peppercorns
6 juniper berries
*120 g rindless smoked streaky
bacon*
3 tbsp oil
grated nutmeg
salt
1 tbsp crème fraîche
1 tsp flour

*Preparation time: 1½ hours
(plus 12 hours marinating time)*

3,400 kJ/810 calories per portion

1 Rinse the rabbit under cold running water, pat dry and cut into portion-sized pieces (*above*). Refrigerate the liver until needed. Put the rabbit pieces in a single layer in a large bowl, add the vermouth, thyme and bay leaf. Peel and finely chop the onion and add to the bowl. Crush the peppercorns and juniper berries with a pestle and mortar, and sprinkle into the marinade. Leave to stand for about 12 hours, turning the meat occasionally.

2 Drain the rabbit through a sieve, reserving the marinade liquid. Pat the meat dry. Finely dice the bacon.

3 Heat the oil in a fireproof casserole and fry the bacon until browned. Add

the rabbit pieces and cook for about 7 minutes until brown all over (*above*). Pour in the marinade and season with nutmeg and salt. Bring to a simmer and cook, uncovered, until the liquid has

reduced by about a third. Reduce the heat to low, cover the pan and cook for about 1 hour.

4 Shortly before the end of the cooking time, crush the rabbit liver with a pestle and mortar (*above*), or purée in a food processor. Stir in the crème fraîche and flour. With a slotted spoon, remove the rabbit pieces from the casserole and transfer them to a warmed serving dish. Stir the liver mixture into the sauce and cook it briefly. Serve the sauce separately accompanied by crusty white bread.

Wine: Choose a dry, not-too-heavy red wine, such as a Côtes-du-Roussillon.

Variation: Lapin à la moutarde
(Rabbit with mustard)
Season a jointed 1.5 kg rabbit with salt and pepper. Place in a greased ovenproof dish and brush with 2 tbsp Dijon mustard. Sprinkle with some chopped thyme and dot with flakes of butter. Cook in an oven preheated to 200°C (400°F or Mark 6) for about 30 minutes, turning once. Add 4 chopped shallots and 10 cl dry white wine and cook for a further 15 minutes. Mix 30 cl crème fraîche with 1 tbsp Dijon mustard, season with salt and pepper and pour over the rabbit. Cover, and cook for a further 5 minutes.

Escalopes de chevreuil

Not difficult • Loire Valley

Venison escalopes with celeriac purée

Serves 4

1 celeriac
salt
6 tbsp double cream
freshly ground black pepper
4 venison escalopes (about 200 g each)
1 tbsp butter
2 tbsp olive oil
4 slices white bread

Preparation time: 30 minutes

1,800 kJ/430 calories per portion

1 Peel, wash and quarter the celeriac. Bring some salted water to the boil in a pan and cook the celeriac until soft, about 20 to 30 minutes. Drain and purée in a food processor, then mix with the cream. Season with salt and pepper and keep warm.

2 Beat the escalopes flat. In a frying pan, heat a little of the butter with the olive oil. Fry the escalopes over high heat for 5 minutes, turning once.

3 Meanwhile, in another pan, heat the remaining butter and fry the bread. Spread with the celeriac purée and arrange in the centre of a warmed serving dish surrounded by the venison.

Wine: Serve a rich red wine from the Loire, such as a Bourgueil or Chinon.

Sauce poivrade

(Pepper sauce)

This sauce is a classic accompaniment to furred game such as venison and rabbit. In a heavy saucepan, brown some game leftovers or trimmings in oil. Add 1 finely chopped carrot and onion. Stir in 3 tbsp wine vinegar, add a bouquet garni and cook until the liquid evaporates.

Meanwhile, in another pan, melt 2 tbsp lard over medium heat, add 1 tbsp flour and stir until brown. Stir in 25 cl meat stock and 2 skinned and seeded tomatoes. Simmer briefly, then rub through a sieve into the pan with the game. Sprinkle with ½ tsp black peppercorns, cover, and simmer for 1 hour. Strain through a sieve, carefully pressing all the juices from the meat and vegetables. Check for seasoning.

Côtelettes de chevreuil

Takes time • Loire Valley   Venison cutlets with grapes   *Serves 4*

40 white grapes
10 cl brandy
Sauce poivrade (opposite page)
8 venison cutlets (about 100 g each)
4 tbsp oil
salt
freshly ground black pepper
20 g butter
8 thin slices French baguette

Preparation time: 2½ hours

2,800 kJ/670 calories per portion

1 Peel and halve the grapes and remove pips, if any. Soak in the brandy for about 2 hours, stirring frequently.

2 Meanwhile, prepare the *Sauce poivrade* (recipe, opposite).

3 Rinse the cutlets under cold running water and pat dry.

4 Heat the oil in a frying pan. Fry the cutlets for about 5 minutes, turning once. Drain, season with salt and pepper and keep warm.

5 Drain the grapes in a colander. Add to the frying pan and cook in the meat juices for about 5 minutes. Remove, drain and reserve.

6 In another frying pan, heat the butter and fry the bread on both sides until golden.

7 Arrange the cutlets on a warmed serving dish with the fried bread. Sprinkle the grapes on top and pour over the *Sauce poivrade.* Serve at once.

Wine: Choose a strong red wine, such as Châteauneuf-du-Pape.

Côtes de sanglier marinées

Wild boar chops *Serves 4*

1 carrot
1 onion
½ litre red Burgundy
1 bouquet garni
1 sage leaf
4 wild boar chops (about 200 g each)
150 g butter
3 tbsp fresh breadcrumbs
1 tbsp flour
1 tbsp brandy
1 garlic clove
1 tsp vinegar
salt

Preparation time: 50 minutes

3,500 kJ/830 calories per portion

1 Peel and slice the carrot. Peel and dice the onion. Pour the wine into a non-reactive pan, add the bouquet garni, sage, carrot and onion. Bring to the boil, then reduce the heat, cover, and simmer for about 20 minutes.

2 Meanwhile, wash and dry the chops. Melt 40 g butter in a sauté pan and fry the chops over high heat for about 5 minutes on each side. Reduce the heat, cover, and cook for a further 5 minutes on each side. Remove and keep warm.

3 Heat 40 g of the remaining butter in the pan and fry the breadcrumbs until golden-brown. Remove and set aside.

4 Remove the bouquet garni from the stock, and purée the vegetables and liquid in a food processor.

5 Melt the remaining butter in the pan. Whisk in the flour and cook until lightly browned, stirring constantly. Continue to stir, adding the puréed stock a little at a time. Add the brandy. Peel and crush the garlic and add to the sauce. Finally add the fried breadcrumbs and the vinegar. Season with salt.

6 Arrange the chops on a warm serving dish. Pour over the sauce. Serve with pasta.

Wine: Serve with the same Burgundy as used to make the sauce.

Note: The French make *mie de pain*, or breadcrumbs, by rubbing white bread, with the crusts cut off, through a fine sieve; they can also be made quickly in a food processor.

Filets de lièvre aux anchois

Fillets of hare with anchovies *Serves 4*

4 hare fillets (about 150 g each)
4 large canned anchovy fillets
salt
freshly ground black pepper
4 garlic cloves
4 large rashers unsalted bacon
2 tbsp oil
3 tbsp tomato purée
4 tbsp dry white wine
¼ litre meat stock
1 egg yolk

Preparation time: 45 minutes

2,300 kJ/550 calories per portion

1 Wash the hare in cold water and pat dry. Drain the anchovies and cut them lengthwise into narrow strips. Using a larding needle, thread the strips at regular intervals through the top of each hare fillet. Season with salt and pepper. Peel and finely chop the garlic and sprinkle over the hare. Wrap a bacon rasher round each fillet.

2 Heat the oil in a sauté pan or deep, heavy frying pan. Sear the fillets over high heat until brown. Reduce the heat and cook for 6 to 8 minutes, basting frequently with the pan juices.

3 Remove the hare from the pan and keep warm. Stir the tomato purée, wine and stock into the pan juices. Add salt and pepper if necessary and skim off surface fat. Remove from the heat and stir in the egg yolk to bind the sauce.

4 Remove the bacon from the fillets and discard. Pour the sauce over the hare and serve with French bread. If you like, garnish with fresh rosemary.

Wine: Serve a Provençal red or rosé, such as a Côtes-de-Provence or the lesser known Bandol or Bellet.

Canard sauvage aux olives

Wild duck with olives

Fairly easy • Provence

Serves 2

1 oven-ready wild duck (about 900 g)
salt
freshly ground black pepper
50 g rindless smoked streaky bacon
70 g sliced white bread
1 egg
1 shallot
6 black olives
4 thin rashers rindless unsmoked
bacon
¼ litre meat stock

Preparation time: 1¾ hours

5,200 kJ/1,200 calories per portion

1 Wash the duck inside and out with cold water. Pat dry, and season with salt and pepper.

2 To make the stuffing, very finely dice the smoked bacon. Soak the bread in lukewarm water, squeeze dry and knead together in a bowl with the diced bacon and the egg. Peel and finely chop the shallot, halve and stone the olives, and mix both into the stuffing. Preheat the oven to 200°C (400°F or Mark 6).

3 Fill the duck with the stuffing. Sew up the body cavity with kitchen twine. Wrap the bacon rashers round the breast, back and thighs. Truss the legs and wings (*see Glossary*).

4 Lay the duck, breast down, in a roasting pan and place in the centre of the oven. After 15 minutes moisten with a little stock if the bacon starts to brown. After another 15 minutes, turn the duck on its back and continue to cook for 45 minutes, basting with the pan juices from time to time.

5 Remove the twine and transfer the duck to a warmed dish surrounded by the bacon rashers. Skim off any fat from the pan juices, stir in the remaining stock and heat through. Carve the duck. Serve with the gravy and fresh bread.

Wine: This dish goes well with a red wine from the Languedoc or Provence.

Cailles en crapaudine

Marinated quail

Fairly easy • Provence

Serves 4

8 oven-ready quail
1 onion
15 g parsley
1 bay leaf
3 tbsp oil
juice of 1 lemon
salt
freshly ground black pepper

*Preparation time: 50 minutes
(plus 2 to 3 hours marinating time)*

1,300 kJ/310 calories per portion

1 Rinse the quail under cold running water, and pat dry. Split the backbone of each bird with poultry shears. Open the bird up and press flat, using the flat of your hand or a meat pounder to break the breastbone.

2 Peel the onion and slice into rings. Wash the parsley, pat dry and chop finely. Place the onion and parsley in a bowl with the bay leaf. Add 2 tbsp of the oil and the lemon juice. Season with salt and pepper. Add the quail, turning to coat it all over. Marinate for at least 2 to 3 hours, turning from time to time.

3 Preheat the oven to 200°C (400°F or Mark 6). Lay the quail in a roasting tin, skin side down, and cook in the top of the oven for about 10 minutes. Turn over, sprinkle with the remaining oil and cook for a further 20 minutes until golden and crisp. Serve with crusty brown bread.

Wine: Serve a light red wine or a rosé from Provence.

Variation: Coat the marinated quail in fresh breadcrumbs before roasting.

Faisan à la crème

Simple • Normandy   **Pheasant with lemon cream sauce**   *Serves 2*

1 oven-ready pheasant (about 800 g)
1 large rasher rindless unsmoked bacon
2 tbsp butter
salt
freshly ground black pepper
grated nutmeg
25 cl cream
juice of 1 lemon

Preparation time: 1¼ hours

4,500 kJ/1,100 calories per portion

1 Wash the pheasant inside and out, and pat dry. Wrap it in the bacon and truss the bird with kitchen twine (*see Glossary*).

2 Melt the butter in a heavy pan or fireproof casserole. Fry the pheasant over high heat until brown on all sides. Season with salt, pepper and nutmeg.

3 Cover the pan and cook over medium heat for about 45 minutes.

4 Transfer the pheasant to a serving dish. Remove the kitchen twine and the bacon. Cut the pheasant in half with poultry shears and keep warm. In the frying pan, fry the bacon until crisp.

5 Stir the cream into the juices in the pan. Add the lemon juice and adjust the seasoning. Pour the sauce over the pheasant and serve at once with the bacon. Unsweetened apple compote and bread are good accompaniments.

Wine: A red Bordeaux, such as a Pomerol, is good with pheasant.

Game birds

Game birds are a French culinary passion. Cooks value them especially for their rich flavours, which differ from region to region with their varied diets, and for the lean, firm meat that results from active lives in the wild. Until recently, few birds at all edible were safe in French skies during the hunting season, from pheasant (*right*), wood-pigeon, wild duck and quail to tiny songbirds such as thrushes and larks.

Now, however, to guard against over-hunting, laws forbid the killing of songbirds and there is a ban on hunting quail. These small, plump birds were once a common sight in the fields of Europe, but wild quail are now scarce. Instead, the birds are farm bred and sold year-round by good butchers and supermarkets. Their meat is tender, with a good flavour, and the French have many delicious ways of cooking them.

Other game birds are also bred for the table. Pheasants specially bred on estates are released into the wild only at the start of the shooting season in October, but successfully retain their distinctive, gamey flavour.

Divers additional flavourings might include wood-pigeons stuffed with raisins soaked in Armagnac, or wild duck cooked with bitter oranges or in a sauce of its own blood, a particular French speciality.

DESSERTS

Following the many and varied delights that comprise the traditional French menu, a selection of cheeses is usually brought to the table. Only a small portion will be taken—just enough to round off the main part of the meal and to accompany what is left of the wine. Then comes the dessert, which should complement what has gone before.

Whatever the degree of richness or complexity, the choice is endless: from the sumptuous confections for which French cuisine is renowned—soufflés, mousses or rich custards and creams—to the magnificent pastries and glazed fruit tarts that are a familiar sight at even the most humble of village patisseries. At more routine family meals, dessert will often consist of just a bowl of fresh fruit or, for example, simple crêpes.

The meal concludes with coffee, drunk strong and from small cups. It may be accompanied by a *digestif*, such as cognac, marc or perhaps a fruit liqueur, and a selection of little fancy biscuits known as *petits fours*.

The French no longer tend to drink sweet wines with dessert. On special occasions champagne or a medium-dry sparkling wine is a popular choice. If you prefer to serve a rich dessert wine, make sure that the dessert is less sweet than the wine itself.

Crêpes Suzette

Pancakes with Grand Marnier

Serves 4

¼ *litre milk*
6 tbsp flour
2 eggs
½ tsp plus 2 tbsp sugar
salt
about 65 g butter
grated rind and juice of 1 unwaxed orange
3 tbsp Grand Marnier

Preparation time: 45 minutes (plus 2 hours standing time)

1,400 kJ/330 calories per portion

1 Warm the milk. Meanwhile, sift the flour into a bowl. Make a well in the centre and break 1 egg into it. Separate the other egg, reserve the white, and add the yolk to the flour. Add ½ tsp sugar and a pinch of salt. Mix together with a wooden spoon. Pour in the milk a little at a time, stirring constantly, until the batter is smooth and runny.

2 Stand the batter in a cool place—not the refrigerator—for about 2 hours. Then, whisk the reserved egg white until it forms stiff peaks and carefully fold it into the batter.

3 Melt a little of the butter in a crêpe pan or in a smooth, non-stick frying pan, spreading the fat thinly and evenly over the bottom. Tipping the pan backwards and forwards, add enough batter to form a paper-thin layer. Fry the pancake, turning once, until lightly browned. Fold in half and in half again, and keep warm. Repeat the process with the rest of the batter.

4 Melt 1 tsp butter in a small frying pan. Do not let it brown. Add 2 tbsp sugar (*above*) and cook slowly until the mixture begins to brown. Add the grated orange rind and juice, stir and heat through, then stir in half the Grand Marnier.

5 Lay the folded pancakes in the small pan, spooning the sauce over them. Slightly warm the rest of the Grand Marnier, pour it over the pancakes and carefully set light to it (*above*).

6 When the flames have died down, arrange the pancakes on very hot plates, pour over the sauce and serve immediately.

Variation: Calvados can be used instead of the Grand Marnier. Or add a dash of kirsch to the batter for extra flavour, then make the pancakes and thinly spread them with apricot jam. Fold over, sprinkle with icing sugar and flambé in a little more kirsch.

Note: For the best results, flambé the pancakes when they are very hot.

Mousse au chocolat

Chocolate mousse

Not difficult • Many regions

Serves 4

150 g plain chocolate
3 egg yolks (see Note)
4 egg whites
1 tsp icing sugar

Preparation time: 20 minutes
(plus 2 hours chilling time)

1,100 kJ/260 calories per portion

1 Break the chocolate into squares, or grate coarsely. Melt gently over a very low heat, preferably in a bowl standing in a pan of gently simmering water.

2 Take off the heat and remove the bowl from the water. Stir the egg yolks into the chocolate. Whisk the egg whites with the icing sugar until stiff. Carefully fold in the chocolate mixture.

3 Transfer the mousse to a serving bowl or individual glasses and chill thoroughly (at least 2 hours). Serve chilled, decorated, if desired, with grated chocolate, chopped pistachio nuts or a little whipped cream.

Variation: To make a mousse without eggs, gently melt 175 g chocolate with 1 to 2 tbsp water in a heavy based pan. Add 75 g icing sugar and 2 tbsp water, and bring to the boil. Remove from the heat and leave to cool completely. Whip 40 cl cold double cream and stir into the chocolate. Serve chilled.

Note: Use only very fresh eggs from a source you trust —uncooked eggs may carry the salmonella bacteria that causes food poisoning.

Crème renversée au caramel

Crème caramel

More complex • Many regions

Serves 4

20 g butter
6 tbsp sugar
4 eggs
1½ tsp vanilla sugar (see Glossary)
40 cl milk

Preparation time: 1 hour
(plus cooling time)

1,300 kJ/310 calories per portion

1 Melt the butter in a saucepan. Add 5 tbsp sugar and 3 tbsp water. Cook over low heat, stirring constantly, until the mixture is a light brown. Do not let it darken too much, otherwise it will taste bitter. Pour the caramel at once into 4 warmed, individual heatproof moulds and rotate the moulds until they are coated with the caramel.

2 Preheat the oven to 180°C (350°F or Mark 4).

3 In a bowl, whisk the eggs with the rest of the sugar and the vanilla sugar until frothy. Bring the milk to the boil and pour it a little at a time into the beaten egg, stirring continuously. Strain the custard through a fine sieve into the prepared moulds.

4 Stand the moulds in a small shallow roasting pan. Fill the pan with hot water two thirds up the sides of the moulds, and cook in the centre of the oven for 25 to 30 minutes, or until set. The custard is set if it stays firm when gently pressed with a finger.

5 Remove the moulds from the pan and allow to cool. With a knife, gently prise the custards away from the edge of the moulds, and turn them out. Add 2 to 3 tbsp water to the moulds and warm through to loosen any caramel sticking to the sides. Pour the caramel over the custards. If you like, chill for a few hours in the refrigerator.

Poires au vin rouge

More complex • Burgundy **Pears in red wine** *Serves 6*

6 firm pears (for example, Williams)
juice of 1 lemon
75 cl red Burgundy (or other
medium red wine)
2 tsp marc or brandy
500 g icing sugar
1 to 2 cinnamon sticks
150 g blackcurrants
150 g redcurrants
200 g raspberries

Preparation time: 1 hour
(plus 2 hours cooling/
chilling time)

2,300 kJ/550 calories
per portion

1 Carefully peel the pears, leaving the stems attached to the fruit. To keep the pears from discolouring, drop them into a bowl of water containing a few drops of the lemon juice.

2 Pour the wine, brandy and ¼ litre water into a heavy saucepan. Stir in 300 g of the icing sugar. Add the cinnamon and bring to the boil. Reduce the heat and add the pears. Simmer for 15 to 20 minutes, gently turning the pears occasionally and basting them with the poaching liquid. The pears are cooked when a skewer can easily be inserted into the base.

3 Meanwhile, wash and stem the blackcurrants and redcurrants (reserving a few for decoration) and hull the raspberries.

4 To make the fruit purée, mix the rest of the icing sugar and lemon juice with 3 tbsp water in another pan and bring to the boil. Reduce the heat and simmer for about 10 minutes. Add the berries and continue to cook for 7 to 8 minutes. Remove, and rub through a sieve.

5 Leave both purée and the pears (in the liquid) to cool at room temperature for about 1 hour. Then place them in the refrigerator for a further hour.

6 To serve, place a helping of purée on each plate. Drain the pears and put them on top, stalks upwards. Decorate with the reserved redcurrants.

Variation: Pears cooked in wine are often served just with their cooking liquid reduced to a syrup.

Clafoutis

Simple • Limousin

Batter pudding with cherries

Serves 4

500 g sweet black or red cherries
3 eggs
2½ tbsp icing sugar
4 tbsp flour
20 cl milk
butter for greasing

Preparation time: 50 minutes
(plus about 30 minutes cooling time)

1,100 kJ/260 calories per portion

1 Preheat the oven to 220°C (425°F or Mark 7). Wash and stone the cherries.

2 Whisk the eggs with 2 tbsp of the icing sugar. Add the flour, then gradually stir in the milk to make a fairly runny batter.

3 Butter an ovenproof baking dish. Arrange the cherries evenly in the dish and pour over the batter. Bake in the centre of the oven for about 20 minutes. Sprinkle the remaining icing sugar over the pudding, and return to the oven for a further 15 minutes, until puffed and browned. Leave the pudding to cool a little and serve warm or cold.

Variation: *Clafoutis*, a speciality of Limousin, is also popular in the rest of France and there are many different versions. It can be made with almost any small, or peeled and cut-up fruit, fresh or dried—for example, apples, strawberries, apricots and prunes.

133

Tarte à l'envers aux abricots

Upside-down apricot tart

More complex • Dauphiné

Serves 6

For the pastry:
200 g flour
1 tsp sugar
100 g butter
salt

For the topping:
750 g fresh apricots
75 g butter
200 g sugar

Preparation time: 1½ hours

2,200 kJ/520 calories per portion

1 Sift the flour into a bowl. Make a well in the centre and add the sugar. Dice the butter and add it to the well. Rub the butter and flour together with your fingers until the mixture has a coarse, mealy texture. Dissolve a pinch of salt in 4 tbsp water and sprinkle the water over the dough, stirring with a knife until it coheres. Gently knead the dough into a ball. Wrap in foil or plastic film and chill for about 20 minutes.

2 Meanwhile, wash, halve and stone the apricots.

3 Grease a 28 cm fireproof gratin dish or flan tin (or a heavy frying pan with a metal or removable handle) with 50 g of the butter. Sprinkle about 100 g sugar in a thick layer over the butter. Arrange the apricot halves, cut side upwards, in tightly packed layers on top of the sugar (*above*).

4 Simmer over low to medium heat on top of the stove, placing a heat-diffusing mat between the burner and the dish if not using a metal pan. When the sugar begins to caramelize—after about 15 to 20 minutes—remove from the heat and allow to cool a little.

5 Preheat the oven to 220°C (425°F or Mark 7). Sprinkle the remaining sugar over the apricots. Cut the remaining butter into slivers and scatter on top.

6 Roll out the dough into a layer about 3 mm thick and lay it on top of the apricots, pressing the edges down into the dish (*above*).

7 Bake in the centre of the oven for 30 to 35 minutes, until golden-brown. Remove and leave for about 10 minutes before carefully turning the tart out on a serving dish. Serve warm with, if you like, crème fraîche or whipped cream.

Variation:

Tarte tatin (Upside-down apple tart) Prepare the dough as above. Peel, core and halve 1 kg small, firm-fleshed, slightly tart apples. Sprinkle 70 g sugar on the base of a fireproof dish or heavy pan and top with 70 g butter cut into slivers. Arrange the apple halves close together, cut side up, on top. Sprinkle with a further 30 g sugar and 30 g butter slivers. Simmer over low to medium heat for 15 to 20 minutes, until the sugar at the bottom has begun to caramelize. Roll out the dough and cover the fruit, as above. Bake in a preheated oven at 220°C (425° F or Mark 7) for about 20 minutes, until golden-brown. Turn out as above.

Far aux raisins

Raisin pudding

Not difficult • Brittany

Serves 4

125 g seedless raisins
10 cl rum
6 eggs
150 g sugar
250 g flour
1 litre milk
about 50 g butter
2 tbsp icing sugar

Preparation time: 1½ hours
(plus 30 minutes soaking time)

4,300 kJ/1,000 calories per portion

1 Soak the raisins in the rum for about 30 minutes.

2 Preheat the oven to 200°C (400°F or Mark 6). Break the eggs into a bowl. Add the sugar and whisk until frothy. Add the flour a little at a time, stirring thoroughly to prevent lumps from forming. Heat the milk and stir it into the mixture.

3 Grease an ovenproof dish with the butter. Pour in ¼ of the batter mixture. Bake in the centre of the oven for about 10 minutes until it begins to set.

4 Remove from the oven. Scatter the raisins over the partly cooked batter. Cover the raisins with the remaining batter and bake for about 50 minutes, until the crust is crisp and golden-brown.

5 Remove the pudding from the oven and sprinkle with icing sugar. Serve warm, straight from the dish.

Note: When made with prunes, this traditional Breton recipe is called *Far breton.*

Calissons d'Aix

Almond biscuits

Fairly easy • Provence

Makes about 20 biscuits

250 g almonds
250 g sugar
4 to 5 tbsp apricot syrup
about 20 rice paper circles
(5 cm in diameter)

For the icing:
1 egg white
100 g icing sugar

Preparation time: 40 minutes

630 kJ/150 calories per biscuit

1 Drop the almonds into boiling water for 1 to 2 minutes. Drain, cool enough to handle and remove the skins. Grind the almonds in a food processor. Mix them with the sugar and stir in the apricot syrup.

2 Gently heat the almond paste in a saucepan. Stir until it begins to go dry. Remove from the heat. Preheat the oven to 200°C (400°F or Mark 6).

3 Lay the rice paper circles on a baking sheet or in shallow tartlet moulds. Place about a teaspoon of paste on each circle. Wet your fingertips in cold water and flatten each one slightly. Leave to cool.

4 Meanwhile, mix together the egg white and the icing sugar, adding a few drops of water if necessary, to make a thickish syrup. Using a pastry brush, coat each biscuit with a little of the syrup.

5 Bake in the centre of the oven for 8 to 10 minutes, until dry and firm.

Note: According to ancient tradition, these biscuits were blessed by the Archbishop of Aix after the Easter mass and distributed at the door of the cathedral. They were believed to provide protection against disease and to stave off epidemics.

Suggested Menus

The menus suggested here are based on recipes from this book. You can also create your own menus by bearing in mind some simple guidelines.

• Avoid serving the same main ingredient for more than one course. For example, if you start with leek and potato soup, do not serve leeks as a vegetable.

• Combine dishes cooked in different ways: for instance, follow boiled fish with roast meat or, if the starter is quiche, do not serve a tart for dessert.

• Suit the number of courses to the number of guests and the occasion. The minimum should be three; the maximum is as many as your culinary skills and your guests' appetites can manage. Ideally, the diners should feel satisfied but not too full to appreciate a dessert or cheese. For menus consisting of many courses, serve only small portions of each dish.

• Bear in mind the amount of effort involved in cooking each dish; if one demands a lot of work, prepare something simpler for the remaining courses.

Everyday menus

Cream of potato soup (*Potage Parmentier*)	26
Chicken with bacon and tomatoes (*Poulet sauté aux lardons*)	109
Cheese or fresh fruit*	—
Crème caramel (*Crème renversée au caramel*)	130
Artichokes with chive dressing (*Artichauts à la ciboulette*)	42
Provençal-style lamb cutlets (*Côtes d'agneau persillées*)	102
Provençal stewed vegetables (*Ratatouille*)	65
Raisin pudding (*Far aux raisins*)	137
Mushrooms in a mustard dressing (*Champignons à la moutarde*)	41
Blanquette of veal (*Blanquette de veau*)	98
Green salad*	—
Batter pudding with cherries (*Clafoutis*)	133
Quiche Lorraine	52
Veal escalopes in shallot sauce (*Escalopes de veau*)	96
Green salad*	—
Fresh fruit*	—
Marrow and leek soup (*Soupe de courge*)	29
Sardines stuffed with spinach (*Sardines farcies aux épinards*)	76
Cheese*	—
Chocolate mousse (*Mousse au chocolat*)	130
Green stuffed eggs (*Œufs durs farcis vert-pré*)	44
Pork escalopes with prunes (*Escalopes aux pruneaux*)	89
Chicory salad*	—
Cheese*	—

Menus based on one substantial dish

Raw vegetables with anchovy dressing (*Crudités à l'anchoïade*)	36
Mediterranean fish stew (*Bouillabaisse*)	72
Cheese*	—
Fruit sorbet*	—
Mushrooms in a mustard dressing (*Champignons à la moutarde*)	41
Garnished sauerkraut (*Choucroute garnie*)	88
Upside-down apricot tart (*Tarte à l'envers aux abricots*)	134
Asparagus with oil and vinegar dressing (*Asperges à la vinaigrette*)	41
Pork pot (*Potée bourguignonne*)	86
Pears in red wine (*Poires au vin rouge*)	132
Chicken or goose liver terrine (*Terrine de foies de volaille*)	48
Pot-roasted stuffed chicken (*Poule au pot farcie*)	110
Cheese and fresh fruit*	—
Nice-style salad (*Salade niçoise*)	44
Stuffed monkfish (*Lotte farcie*)	75
Batter pudding with cherries (*Clafoutis*)	133

Intimate dinner parties for 2 to 4

Crawfish in red wine (*Civet de langouste*)	69
Roast pigeon (*Pigeons rôtis*)	115
Seasonal vegetables*	—
Cheese*	—
Sorbet*	—
Asparagus with oil and vinegar dressing (*Asperges à la vinaigrette*)	41
Sole in white wine (*Filets de sole à la bretonne*)	74
Marinated quail (*Cailles en crapaudine*)	123
Fresh fruit*	—
Scallops in cream sauce (*Coquilles Saint-Jacques*)	68
Lamb chops with fresh mint (*Tranches de gigot à la menthe*)	100
Mixed salad*	—
Pancakes with Grand Marnier (*Crêpes Suzette*)	129
Mixed hors-d'œuvre (*Hors-d'œuvre varié*)*	—
Pheasant with lemon cream sauce (*Faisan à la crème*)	124
Puréed celery or green beans*	—
Pears in red wine (*Poires au vin rouge*)	132
Fish terrine (*Terrine de poisson*)	38
Fillet steak in Chablis sauce (*Steak du Morvan*)	93
Upside-down apricot tart (*Tarte à l'envers aux abricots*)	134

Menus for 6 to 8

Chicken or goose liver terrine (*Terrine de foies de volaille*)	48
Chicken in red wine (*Coq au vin*)	106
Green salad*	—
Cheese*	—
Chocolate mousse (*Mousse au chocolat*)	130
Raw vegetables with anchovy dressing (*Crudités à l'anchoïade*)	36
Pot-roasted beef in red wine (*Bœuf en daube*)	94
Fresh noodles*	—
Upside-down apple tart (*Tarte tatin*)	134
Fish terrine (*Terrine de poisson*)	38
Roast leg of lamb (*Gigot à l'auvergnate*)	100
Potato gratin (*Gratin dauphinois*)	58
Pears in red wine (*Poires au vin rouge*)	132
Snails in herb sauce (*Escargots aux fines herbes*)	61
Trout in vermouth (*Truites Mont-Dore*)	79
Green salad*	—
Fresh fruit*	—
Cream of potato soup (*Potage Parmentier*)	26
Salmon with shallots (*Saumon aux échalotes*)	83
Cheese*	—
Sorbets*	—
Leek flan (*Flan bourguignon*)	55
Wild duck with olives (*Canard sauvage aux olives*)	123
Green salad*	—
Fruit salad*	—

Vegetarian menus

Pumpkin soup (*Soupe au potiron*)	29
Leek flan (*Flan bourguignon*)	55
Provençal stewed vegetables (*Ratatouille*)	65
Crème caramel (*Crème renversée au caramel*)	130
Cream of potato soup (*Potage Parmentier*)	26
Artichokes with chive dressing (*Artichauts à la ciboulette*)	42
Cheese soufflé (*Soufflé au fromage*)	55
Green salad*	—
Upside-down apricot tart (*Tarte à l'envers aux abricots*)	134
Asparagus with oil and vinegar dressing (*Asperges à la vinaigrette*)	41
Tomato omelette (*Omelette de tomates*)	56
Marrow gratin (*Gratin de courge*)	65
Green salad*	—
Batter pudding with cherries (*Clafoutis*)	133

Green stuffed eggs (*Œufs durs farcis vert-pré*)	44
Potato gratin (*Gratin dauphinois*)	58
Mixed salad*	—
Cheese*	—
Upside-down apple tart (*Tarte tatin*)	134

Menus for special occasions

Asparagus with oil and vinegar dressing (*Asperges à la vinaigrette*)	41
Crayfish gratin (*Gratin de queues d'écrevisses*)	70
Duck with orange sauce (*Canard à la bigarade*)	113
Selection of cheeses*	—
Pears in red wine (*Poires au vin rouge*)	132
with Sorbet balls*	—
Coffee and Almond biscuits (*Calissons d'Aix*)	137
Crayfish bisque (*Bisque d'écrevisses*)	30
Sole in white wine (*Filets de sole à la bretonne*)	74
Guinea fowl with morels (*Pintade aux morilles*)	112
Selection of cheeses*	—
Upside-down apricot tart (*Tarte à l'envers aux abricots*)	134
Coffee and cognac or liqueurs*	—
Beef consommé with cheese puffs (*Consommé aux profiteroles*)	32
Pike in cream sauce (*Brochet à la crème*)	80
Roast pigeon (*Pigeons rôtis*)	115
Cheese*	—
Upside-down apple tart (*Tarte tatin*)	134
Coffee and cognac or liqueurs*	—
Fish terrine (*Terrine de poisson*)	38
Morels in cream sauce (*Croûtes aux morilles*)	62
Wild boar chops (*Côtes de sanglier marinées*)	120
Green salad*	—
Sorbets*	—
Coffee and *petits fours**	—
Beef consommé with cheese puffs (*Consommé aux profiteroles*)	32
Scallops in cream sauce (*Coquilles Saint-Jacques*)	68
Venison cutlets with grapes (*Cotelettes de chevreuil*)	119
Chestnut purée or green salad*	—
Selection of cheeses*	—
Pancakes with Grand Marnier (*Crêpes Suzette*)	129
Coffee	—

*Recipes for simple dishes such as a green salad are not included in the book. Items marked with an * are available from well-stocked supermarkets, delicatessens or good patisseries.*

Glossary

This glossary is intended as a brief guide to some less familiar cookery terms and ingredients, including words and items found on French menus.

Aïoli: a garlic sauce with the consistency of mayonnaise; served with vegetables, saltwater fish and hard-boiled eggs

Argenteuil, à l': a name for various dishes containing asparagus

Bain-marie (also called water bath): a large pot or vessel in which water is boiled so that a smaller vessel can be placed inside and its contents cooked or heated. It is used for making custards, creams and other preparations that cannot tolerate direct heat.

Bard: to cover meat, poultry, game and sometimes fish with thin strips of pork fat or bacon before roasting or braising

Béarnaise: a type of sauce made with shallots, egg, white wine, vinegar, tarragon and butter; it accompanies meat, fish and egg dishes.

Béchamel: a basic white sauce, made with butter, flour and milk, often seasoned with nutmeg

Beurre blanc: a piquant sauce often served with poached fish. Butter is whipped into shallots that have been cooked in wine vinegar or white wine until the liquid has almost evaporated.

Beurre manié: a paste made from equal quantities of flour and butter, used for thickening or binding sauces

Bisque: a cream soup usually made from shellfish such as lobster or crayfish

Blanch: to plunge food into boiling water for a short period; it helps to remove strong flavours and softens vegetables before further cooking.

Blanquette: a stew of veal, lamb or chicken in a cream sauce

Blind-baking: a technique for baking unfilled pastry cases for flans or quiches to ensure thorough cooking. The pastry base is pricked all over with a fork, lined with greaseproof paper and weighted with dry beans or peas. It is baked for 10 to 15 minutes; then beans and paper are removed and the filling added for cooking.

Bonne femme: literally "housewife style"; a name given to dishes served with diced potatoes, carrots and onions sautéed in butter.

Bordelaise: a name given to dishes served with a sauce made from brown stock, red wine and bone marrow

Bouquet garni: a bundle of several herbs—the classic three are bay leaf, thyme and parsley—tied together and used to flavour a stock or stew. The bouquet garni is removed and discarded at the end of the cooking time.

Bretonne, à la: literally "Brittany style"; a name given to dishes that usually include fresh white beans; fish *à la bretonne*, however, is braised with a vegetable and cream or wine sauce.

Brie: a round, soft cheese from Champagne

Brioche: a bun made from very light, buttery yeast dough

Calvados: an apple brandy distilled from cider in the Calvados area of Normandy

Camembert: a soft unpressed cheese, originally from Normandy, with a bloomy rind and creamy texture

Canapé: an hors-d'œuvre made from small, crustless slices of bread or toast, spread with savoury toppings

Cantal: a nutty-flavoured hard cheese from the Auvergne, also used for cooking

Caramelize: to heat sugar, or a food naturally rich in sugar such as fruit, until the sugar turns brown and syrupy

Cassoulet: a haricot bean stew made with meat, goose or duck, from the Languedoc and southwest France

Chantilly: lightly whipped cream

Chiffonnade: any green leafy herb or vegetable—especially lettuce, spinach, chard or sorrel—that has been cut into very fine ribbons. They can be used as a raw garnish or in salads, or sautéed in butter to garnish a soup.

Chili peppers: a variety of hot red or green peppers. They contain volatile oils that can irritate the skin and eyes and must be handled with caution. Wash hands immediately after using them.

Cidre: cider. Most French cider comes from Normandy and Brittany and varies in taste and alcoholic content. *Cidre doux* (sweet) and *cidre brut* (dry) are both available in still and sparkling—*cidre bouché*—versions.

Cognac: a high-quality grape brandy from the area around the town of the same name. Good cognac is considered the finest brandy in the world. Cognac can also be used to flavour sauces, desserts and meat pâtés.

Compote: fresh or dried fruits cooked and served in a flavoured sugar syrup

Comté: a hard cheese from the French Alps, similar to Swiss Emmenthal

Confit: duck, goose or pork, salted, cooked and preserved in its own fat

Crécy, à la: a name for various dishes, all of which contain carrots

Crème de cassis: a liqueur made from blackcurrants. With champagne it makes *kir royale*; with dry white wine, *kir*.

Crème fraîche: a slightly ripened, sharp-tasting French double cream containing about 35 per cent fat

Crêpe: a paper-thin pancake that can accommodate sweet or savoury fillings

Croustade: a flaky, puff or short pastry case stuffed with a savoury filling. It is also the name for a hollowed-out bread case, brushed with egg and deep-fried.

Croûtons: cubes or slices of white bread fried in butter or toasted, served as a garnish for soup

Dijon mustard: a smooth or grainy hot mustard; may be flavoured with herbs, green peppercorns or white wine

Dress: to prepare meat, poultry, game or fish for cooking, such as by cleaning, trimming or gutting

Duchesse, à la: a method of preparing potatoes, which are mashed with egg yolks and piped as a garnish

Eau-de-vie: a distilled wine or clear spirit distilled from fruit or grain

Farce: a mixture of various chopped ingredients used for stuffing pastry, fish, meat or vegetables

Fines herbes: a mixture of finely chopped fresh herbs, the classic herbs being parsley, chives, tarragon and chervil. In France the term sometimes applies to chopped parsley alone.

Flambé: to pour alcoholic spirit such as brandy or calvados over meat or desserts, and ignite it. The alcohol burns away, leaving its flavour.

Fond: a French term for stock

Fricassée: a braised dish in which the cooking liquid is thickened with a mixture of egg and cream

Fruits de mer: literally, "fruits of the sea"; a mixture of crustaceans and other shellfish, often served as an hors-d'œuvre

Fumet: a concentrated broth extracted from fish, meat or vegetables by slow cooking

Galantine: a name for various dishes made from poultry or meat, which are first boned and stuffed, then pressed into a symmetrical roll and cooked in stock. Served cold, they are often garnished with aspic.

Galette: a large, flat, round cake, made from flaky, unleavened or yeast dough

Glace de viande: a concentrated meat glaze achieved by boiling meat stock to a sticky consistency.

Grand Marnier: a high-quality liqueur made from cognac and orange peel, which has a distinctive orange flavour

Gratin: a baked dish with a crunchy topping of breadcrumbs or grated cheese that has been browned in the oven or under the grill

Hollandaise: a sauce of egg yolks, butter and lemon juice, served with eggs, fish or vegetables

Julienne: the French term for vegetables or other foods cut into thin strips

Macedoine: a mixture of raw or cooked vegetables or fruits, served hot or cold

Maison: literally "house"; added to the name of a dish, it means cooked to the special recipe of the restaurant.

Marc: a potent brandy distilled from the residue of grapes after pressing

Marinade: a seasoning mixture to coat or soak meat or fish before cooking in order to tenderize or impart flavour. A wet marinade is usually made from oil, herbs, vegetables and seasoning mixed with wine, vinegar or lemon juice; a dry marinade consists of a mixture of salt, herbs and spices.

Marmite: a term now used for a deep metal or earthenware stew-pot. Traditionally, it is a tall, wide, covered pot made of earthenware, glazed on the inside so as not to absorb fat, but unglazed on the outside to absorb heat more readily.

Matelote: strictly, a dish consisting of freshwater fish stewed in red or white wine; *Matelote à la normande,* however, is made from saltwater fish.

Mie de pain: the centre of a loaf, without the crust; it is rubbed through a sieve and used for binding soups and sauces.

Mirepoix: a mixture of finely chopped sautéed vegetables (usually onion, carrot and celery, sometimes with the addition of chopped ham and herbs) that is used as a foundation for soups, sauces and stews.

Miroton: a type of meat stew with onions

Monkfish (also called angler-fish): an Atlantic fish with a scaleless, thick-skinned body and an enormous, ugly head. Only the tail portion is edible.

Morels: wild mushrooms with brown, pitted caps. Dried morels should be soaked in water or milk before use.

Mornay sauce: a *béchamel* sauce with the addition of cheese

Mousse: a general term for a cold savoury or sweet dish with a light creamy texture. Sweet mousses are traditionally composed of a flavoured base aerated with beaten egg whites, whipped cream, or both; gelatine is sometimes used as a setting agent.

Mousseline: a term for various dishes and sauces that have been prepared with whipped cream; also applied to light, airy cakes or pastries such as, for example, *brioche mousseline*. It is also a term for a delicate fish or meat forcemeat.

Niçoise, à la: a name for various dishes prepared with tomatoes and usually also garlic

Non-reactive pan or bowl: a cooking vessel whose surface does not react chemically with food. Materials used include ovenproof clay, stainless steel, enamel, glass and non-stick finishes. Untreated cast-iron and aluminium may react with acids, producing discoloration or a peculiar taste.

Papillote: a paper case for wrapping food during cooking

Pâté: a meat, fish or vegetable paste. Strictly, the name refers to such a dish baked in a pastry case; however, it is often also used to refer to a terrine. *See also* Terrine.

Petits-fours: small fancy biscuits, such as macaroons, or small cakes dipped in fondant icing

Potée: a name originally given to meat and vegetable dishes cooked in an earthenware pot; it refers especially to pork cooked with cabbage, potatoes and other vegetables.

Pré-salé: a term describing the meat of sheep and lambs that graze on salt meadows close to the sea

Provençale, à la: a name for various dishes prepared with tomatoes and garlic

Quatre-épices: a blend of spices—black pepper, cloves, nutmeg and ginger—available from many greengrocers

Ragout: a well-seasoned stew of meat, poultry or fish

Rice paper: a thin, translucent, edible paper made from rice, used as a base for biscuits, cakes or confectionary

Roquefort: a blue-veined cheese from the town of the same name, made from ewe's milk and matured in limestone caves

Rôti: a joint for roasting, or roast meat

Roux: a mixture of butter and flour used to thicken sauces. After the mixture has cooked gently, a liquid is added to it.

Scorzonera: a thin, long cylindrical root with brown or blackish skin, similar in shape and taste to salsify

Shallot: a mild variety of onion, with a subtle flavour and papery, red-brown skin. If shallots are unavailable, substitute spring onions in a recipe.

Soufflé: a fluffy sweet or savoury dish made from egg yolks and stiffly-beaten egg whites

Tarte: an open pie or tart, usually filled with fruit

Terrine: a meat, fish or vegetable loaf, or the dish in which it is cooked in the oven, often submerged in a water bath. *See also* Pâté.

Timbale: a small, mostly drum-shaped, baking dish or individual mould, or its contents, either a creamy bake of vegetables, meat or fish, or a savoury stuffing in a pastry shell.

Truss: to secure the wings and legs of a bird against its body. This can be done by tying or sewing them with cotton or kitchen twine. The wings may also be tucked back under the bird.

Vanilla sugar: a flavoured sugar used in desserts. To make at home, place a vanilla pod in a jar of caster sugar, close tightly and leave for a week or more; the longer it is left, the stronger the flavour. It is also sold ready made.

Velouté: literally "rich and velvety"; a white sauce made from a *roux* of flour and butter plus poultry, veal or fish stock

Vinaigrette: a dressing of oil and vinegar mixed with salt and pepper, and other seasonings such as mustard and herbs

CONVERSION CHART

These figures are not exact equivalents, but have been rounded up or down slightly to make measuring easier.

Weight Equivalents			Volume Equivalents	
Metric	Imperial		Metric	Imperial
15 g	½ oz		8 cl	3 fl oz
30 g	1 oz		12.5 cl	4 fl oz
60 g	2 oz		15 cl	¼ pint
90 g	3 oz		17.5 cl	6 fl oz
125 g	¼ lb		25 cl	8 fl oz
150 g	5 oz		30 cl	½ pint
200 g	7 oz		35 cl	12 fl oz
250 g	½ lb		45 cl	¾ pint
350 g	¾ lb		50 cl	16 fl oz
500 g	1 lb		60 cl	1 pint
1 kg	2 to 2¼ lb		1 litre	35 fl oz

Cover: Pieces of chicken are cooked in a generous amount of red Burgundy wine to impart a rich colour and flavour to *Coq au vin* (*recipe, page 106*). Mushrooms, smoked bacon and spring onions—used here instead of the more traditional shallots—give the dish substance. To make the meal complete, all that is needed is some crusty French bread and a glass of red wine, followed by a selection of French cheeses.

TIME-LIFE BOOKS

COOKERY AROUND THE WORLD
English edition staff for *France*
Editorial: Ilse Gray, Luci Collings,
Tim Cooke
Design: Paul Reeves
Production: Emma Wishart, Theresa John
Technical Consultant: Michael A. Barnes

English translation by Isabel Varea for
Ros Schwartz Translations, London

© 1994 Gräfe und Unzer Verlag GmbH,
Munich: *Küchen der Welt: Frankreich*

This edition published by Time-Life Books
B.V. Amsterdam
Authorized English language edition
© 1994 Time-Life Books B.V.
First English language printing 1994

TIME-LIFE is a trademark of Time Warner
Inc. U.S.A.

ISBN 0 7054 1197 4

Colour reproduction by Fotolito Longo, Bolzano, Italy
Typeset by A. J. Latham Limited, Dunstable, Bedfordshire, England
Printed and bound by Mondadori, Verona, Italy

GRÄFE UND UNZER

EDITORS: Dr. Stephanie von Werz-Kovacs and Birgit Rademacker
Sub-Editor: Anita Tafferner
Designer: Konstantin Kern
Recipes tested by: Marianne Obermayr
Production:
BuchHaus Kraxenberger.Gigler.GmbH
Cartography: Huber, Munich

Susi Piroué, who lives in Germany and works in the book trade, has for many years been involved with cookery and wine books, both as author and editor. Her passion for French cuisine began when she married into a French family. At home, she prefers to cook in the French style and for this book has chosen only authentic French recipes.

Michael Brauner, who photographed the food for this volume, is a graduate of the Berlin Fotoschule. He worked as an assistant to several French and German photographers and specialized in food photography for five years before setting up on his own in 1984. He now divides his time between his studios in Munich, Karlsruhe and Gordes in Provence.

Detlef Kellermann is a freelance artist and illustrator based in Aachen who exhibits both in Germany and abroad. A versatile artist, he works in many different materials and styles; apart from illustrations, he has, for example, designed stage sets and created mosaic structures. The watercolours in this book reflect his love for France and its people.

Picture Credits

Colour illustrations: Detlef Kellermann

All photographs were taken by Michael Brauner, Food Fotografie, unless indicated below:

Cover: Graham Kirk, London; 4-5, clockwise from top left: Harald Mante, Dortmund (garden, Château Villandry); Bildagentur J. Dziemballa, Poblete, Munich (flower meadow, Brittany); Martin Thomas, Aachen-Alt Lemiers (grape harvest in Roussillon, game of boules and Burgundy canal); Robert Gigler, Munich (old laundry, Vannes); Wilfried Becker, Vaterstetten/Munich (pavement café, St. Tropez); 8-9: Bildagentur J. Dziemballa, Poblete, Munich (Château de la Bretesche, Brittany); 10 (2): real-bild Klaus-D. Neumann, Munich; 11: Herbert Hartmann, Munich; 12, top: Armin Faber, Mühlheim; 12, bottom: AV-Bilderbank Lothar Schiffler, Munich; 13: Werner Neumeister, Munich; 14, top: Martin Thomas, Aachen-Alt Lemiers; 14, bottom: AV-Bilderbank Lothar Schiffler, Munich; 15: Gerhard P. Müller, Dortmund; 16: Josef Bieker, Dortmund; 17, Martin Thomas, Aachen-Alt Lemiers; 18: Josef Bieker, Dortmund; 19, top: Heinz Wohner, Dortmund; 19, bottom: Robert Gigler, Munich; 20, top: Heinz Wohner, Dortmund; 20, bottom: Robert Gigler, Munich; 21, top: Werner Neumeister, Munich; 21, bottom: Martin Thomas, Aachen-Alt Lemiers; 22, top: Werner Neumeister, Munich; 22, bottom: Robert Gigler, Munich; 23 (2): AV-Bilderbank Lothar Schiffler, Andreani, Munich; 43: Heinz Wohner, Dortmund; 47: Fotostudio Teubner, Füssen; 79, 110, 125: Reinhard-Tierfoto, Heiligkreuzsteinach.